A REGISTRY
of WOMEN
in RELIGIOUS STUDIES

A REGISTRY
of WOMEN
in RELIGIOUS STUDIES

1981-82 EDITION

Compiled by
Carole R. Bohn
and Lorine Getz

THE EDWIN MELLEN PRESS
NEW YORK AND TORONTO

Studies in Women and Religion, Supplementary volume one

ISBN 0-88946-277-1

Studies in Women and Religion ISBN 0-88946-549-5

Copyright ©️ *1981, The Edwin Mellen Press*

For Information:

The Edwin Mellen Press
P.O. Box 450
Lewiston, New York 14092

PRINTED IN THE UNITED STATES OF AMERICA

CONTENTS

FOREWORD

The 1981-82 edition of the Registry of Women in Religious Studies is the fourth edition of this publication originally published in 1972 by the Women's Caucus: Religious Studies of the American Academy of Religion. It contains a listing of women in academic religion who submitted their names during the spring and summer of 1980. Although it does not include all women in the various disciplines of Religious Studies and does not attempt to give exhaustive information on each participant, this Registry provides basic information in a concise form and thus is a helpful reference source.

Two earlier editions of the Registry were jointly published by the Women's Caucus: Religious Studies of the American Academy of Religion and the Doctoral Placement Service, Women's Theological Coalition, Boston Theological Institute. With this edition, we enter a new phase. Still compiled through joint efforts of the Women's Caucus and the Women's Theological Coalition, the Registry is now scheduled to be published biannually. Data for this issue was gathered in the spring of 1980 to be published in early 1981; information will be collected for the next issue in the spring of 1982 to be published in early 1983; and so on. In this manner updated listings will be provided on a regular basis.

The Registry has several main sections: descriptions of the Doctoral Placement Service for Women and the Women's Caucus; an alphabetical listing of basic information on women in religious studies; and an index by field.

Those women who would like to be listed in the next edition should send the appropriate information (see form on last page) to The Edwin Mellen Press for inclusion in the 1983-84 edition. Additional copies of the 1981-82 Registry of Women in Religious Studies may be obtained from:

The Edwin Mellen Press
P.O. Box 450
Lewiston, N.Y. 14092

Carole R. Bohn, co-editor   Lorine M. Getz, co-editor
Women's Theological Coalition   Women's Caucus:
Boston Theological Institute   Religious Studies

A NOTE ABOUT THE WOMEN'S CAUCUS:
RELIGIOUS STUDIES

The Women's Caucus: Religious Studies grew out of a task force within the American Academy of Religion. It was organized to facilitate exchange among academic women in the field, to promote research and teaching opportunities, and to encourage the visibility and audibility of professional women engaged in the study and teaching of religion.

A quarterly Newsletter is the medium of contact and exchange among members of the Caucus. The Newsletter contains information on the local, regional, national, and international activities of women in the field of religion as well as on matters of technical interest, e.g., dissertation research and abstracts, syllabi of courses on the subject of women, bibliographies, academic openings, grants and fellowships, etc.

Full membership in the Caucus includes subscription to the Newsletter and listing in the Registry, which is published jointly with the Doctoral Placement Service for Women in Religious Studies, Women's Theological Coalition.

The Caucus holds its annual meeting during the joint convention of the American Academy of Religion and the Society of Biblical Literature.

For information on the Women's Caucus: Religious Studies contact co-chairs:

Lorine Getz
Boston Theological Institute
210 Herrick Road
Newton Centre, MA 02159

Rosemary Radford Ruether
Garrett-Evangelical
Theological Seminary
2121 Sheridan Road
Evanston, IL 60201

Materials for the Newsletter should be submitted to the editor:

Karen A. Barta
826 N. 14th Street, #309
Milwaukee, WI 53233

A NOTE ABOUT THE DOCTORAL PLACEMENT SERVICE
FOR WOMEN IN RELIGIOUS STUDIES

The Doctoral Placement Service for Women in Religious Studies was organized by the Women's Theological Coalition of the Boston Theological Institute in 1972. Under a grant from the Ford Foundation, the Service worked toward increased placement of women scholars.

In 1980 the referral service of the DPS was discontinued under the terms of the Ford grant. The newsletter of the DPS, however, has been continued and expanded to list not only positions in higher education, but those in specialized ministries as well.

The Placement News is published bi-monthly from September to May with listings of teaching positions, administrative posts, and specialized ministry positions (such as campus ministry, hospital chaplaincy, counseling, etc.). The subscription rate is $5.00 per year for five issues.

Individuals and institutions wishing to subscribe to The Placement News or organizations wishing to advertise openings (for which there is no charge) should write to:

The Placement News
c/o BTI
210 Herrick Road
Newton, MA 02159

DIRECTORY OF WOMEN IN RELIGIOUS STUDIES, 1981-82

The following pages list the names, addresses and available professional data of women in Religious Studies who submitted materials during the Spring and Summer 1980 for this publication. Entries are given according to the following model:

NAME
  -Address
  -Phone number
  -Religious affiliation
  -Major area(s) of competence
  -Latest Degree
  -Thesis
  -Publications, research area(s)
  -Present position

A

AGNEW, Mary Barbara
  -214 Ashwood Rd.
  Villanova, PA 19085
  -PhD
  -Sacraments, Socio-Cultural
  Foundations of Religion
  -Asst. Prof., Villanova Univ.

AHL, Sally W.
  -909 College
  Tarkio, MO 64491
  -(816) 736-5565
  -Old Testament, Mediterranean
  Studies
  -PhD, Brandeis Univ., 1973
  -Thesis: Epistolary Texts from
  Ugarit
  -Course Handbook: Acts of God
  and Man in the Old Testament;
  Linguistic Analysis applied to
  the Hebrew text (in light of

AHL, (cont.)
  Semitic languages); Sociologi-
  cal Studies related to OT
  Society-Culture
  -Assoc. Prof. of Religion,
  Tarkio College

ALBANESE, Catherine L.
  -Dept. of Religion
  Wright State Univ.
  Dayton, OH 45435
  -(513) 873-2273
  -History of Religions: American
  Religious History, Late 18th
  and antebellum 19th centuries
  -PhD, Univ. of Chicago, 1972
  -Son of the Fathers: The Civil
  Religion of the American Revo-
  lution; Corresponding Motion:
  Transcendental Religion and the
  New America; America: Religions
  and Religion (forthcoming)
  -Assoc. Prof., Religion,
  Wright State Univ.

ALPERN, Barbara D.
  -Foxridge Apts., #700F
  Blacksburg, VA 24060
  -(703) 552-3482
  -Philosophy of Religion, Reli-
  gious Language
  -PhD, Univ. of Pittsburgh, 1980
  -Thesis: Pannenberg on Analogy
  -Religion and Literature
  -Asst. Prof., Radford Univ.

ALPERT, Rebecca Trachtenberg
-6901 Old York Rd., C212
Philadelphia, PA 19126
-(215) 927-6068
-Jewish
-Judaica, American Religion
-PhD, Temple Univ., 1978
-Contemporary Jewish Studies,
Role of Rabbi, Women in Judaism,
"Regina Jonas -- 'First Woman
Rabbi'"
-Dir. of Student Affairs,
P.T. Instr., Reconstructionist
Rabbinical College

ANDA, Eva
-762 Birch Walk, Apt. H
Goleta, CA 93017
-Hellenistic Christianity, Women
in Religion
-PhD, Univ. of California,
Santa Barbara, pending

ANDOLSEN, Barbara Hilkert
-400 Central Park W., #17C
New York, NY 10025
-(212) 666-1202
-Roman Catholic
-Ethics, Women in Religion
-PhD, Vanderbilt Univ., 1981
-Thesis: Racism in the 19th and
20th Century Feminist Movements
-Feminist Ethics, Business Ethics

ATHANS, Mary Christine, BVM
-School of Theology at Claremont
1325 N. College Ave.
Claremont, CA 91711
-(714) 626-3521 x221
-Roman Catholic
-History of Christian Thought,
Contemporary (American) Reli-
gious Thought, Judaica, Jewish-
Christian Relations
-Thesis: Theo. Roots of American
Anti-Semitism -- 1900-1970
-Ecumenics, Jewish-Christian
Relations, Comparison of Jews,

ATHANS, (cont.)
Catholics and Protestants at
specific points in American
History
-Asst. Academic Dean;
Instr., Theology and Ecumenics,
School of Theology at Claremont

ATKINSON, Clarissa Webster
-343 South Ave.
Weston, MA 02193
-(617) 899-3823
-Episcopal
-Church History, History of
Christian Thought, Medieval,
Reformation
-PhD, Boston College, 1979
-Thesis: "This Creature": A Study
of the Book of Margery Kempe
-Christian Attitudes toward the
Family, Women, Sexuality in the
late Medieval and Reformation
Period
-Asst. Prof.,
History of Christianity
Harvard Divinity School

BABINSKI, Jeri Drum
-12 Longmeadow Rd.
Westboro, MA 01581
-(617) 366-2803
-United Church of Christ
-Psychology of Religion, Pastoral
Counseling, Clinical Pastoral
Education
-D.Min., Andover Newton Theo.
School, 1976
-Thesis: A Study of Transforma-
tion in the Pastoral Counseling
Process
-Protestant Chaplain,
CPE Supervisor,
Westboro State Hospital

BABINSKI, (cont.)
Adjunct faculty,
Andover Newton Theo. School

BAILEY-ADAMS, Marcy
-215 Herrick Rd.
Newton Centre, MA 02159
-(617) 969-8754
-United Church of Christ
-Old Testament, Religion and
Culture, Feminism
-M. Div., Andover Newton Theo.
School, 1980
-Editor, Affirmations (1978-79),
BTI newsletter
-Literary Criticism, Sociology,
Anthropology, and Liberation
Theology
-Admin. Asst., Lesley College
School for Children

BANCROFT, Nancy
-5980 Woodbine Ave.
Philadelphia, PA 19131
-(215) 473-4750
-Ethics and Sociology of Reli-
gion, Social Ethics, Religion
and Society
-PhD, Harvard Univ., 1977
-Religion and Social Change,
Christianity and Marxism
-Asst. Prof., Lincoln Univ.

BARSTOW, Anne
-606 W. 122 St.
New York, NY 10027
-(212) 662-8209
-Protestant
-Church History, Medieval,
Women's History
-PhD, Columbia Univ., 1978
-Thesis: Defense of Clerical
Marriage: 11th Century
-Churches' Attitudes toward
Clerical Wives, European Witch-
craft Persecutions
-Assoc. Prof.,
SUNY at Old Westbury

BARTA, Karen A.
-826 N. 14th St., #309
Milwaukee, WI 53233
-Roman Catholic
-New Testament
-PhD, Marquette Univ., 1979
-Thesis: Mission and Discipleship
in Matthew: A Redactional-
Critical Study of MT 10:34
-Exegesis of the Gospel of
Matthew
-Asst. Prof., Sacred Heart
School of Theo., Hales Corners

BASS, Dorothy C.
-5427 S. Kenwood Ave.
Chicago, IL 60615
-(312) 363-5026
-United Church of Christ
-History of Religion: North
American
-PhD., Brown Univ., 1980
-Articles on Women and Religion,
Free Thought
-Instr., Humanities,
Univ. of Chicago

BASU, Patricia Lyons
-1320 S. Williams Circle
Elizabeth City, NC 27909
-(919) 338-1996
-History of Asian Religions,
Hinduism
-PhD, Princeton Univ., 1978
-Thesis: A Study of Hindu Con-
cept of Vāk: The Power of the
Word in an Oral Society
-Feminism and Religion
-Instr., Social Science,
Elizabeth City State Univ.

BELMONTE, Frances
-1325 Jefferson Ave.
Memphis, TN 38104
-(901) 725-6761
-Roman Catholic
-Systematic/Historical Theology
-PhD, Boston College/Andover
Newton Theo. School, 1980
-Thesis: Reconciliation: A
Participative Theology

BELMONTE, (cont.)
-Res. Theologian,
Diocese of Memphis

BIRNBAUM, Ruth
-132 Groveland St.
Springfield, MA 01108
-(413) 737-8161
-Judaica, Jewish Philosophy
-PhD, Boston Univ., expected 1981
-Thesis: Jewish Medieval Aristo-
telianism
-Seeking Employment

BLOOMQUIST, Karen L.
-146-19 175th St.
Springfield Gardens, NY 11434
-(212) 723-1792
-Lutheran (ALC)
-Contemporary Religious Thought,
Systematics, Liberation The-
ology and Ethics
-PhD, Union Theo. Sem., NYC,
expected 1982
-Feminist Theology in Relation
to Parish Ministry, Working
Class Experience

BOHN, Carole R.
-33 Kingston St.
Somerville, MA 02144
-(617) 666-9569
-Pastoral Psychology/Pastoral
Practical, Counseling Women,
Supervision
-EdD, Boston Univ., 1981
-Thesis: An Empirical Study of
Women in Theological Education
-Coordinator,
Women's Theo. Coalition,
Boston Theo. Institute

BORCHERT, Doris Ann
-North American Baptist Sem.
1605 S. Euclid Ave.
Sioux Falls, SD 57105
-M.RE, Children's Work and
Teaching Methods
-Instr., Christian Education,
North American Baptist Sem.

BOUCHER, Madeleine
-158 N. Broadway, 2E
White Plains, NY 10603
-(914) 761-6525
-Roman Catholic
-New Testament
-PhD, Brown Univ., 1973
-The Mysterious Parable: A Lit-
erary Study
-Women in New Testament, Gospel
of Mark
-Assoc. Prof., Dept. of Theology,
Fordham Univ.

BOYD, Sandra H.
-263 Payson Rd.
Belmont, MA 02178
-(617) 489-2829
-Episcopal
-History of Religions, American
Religious History
-M.Div., Episcopal Divinity
School, 1978
-Women in American Religious
History
-Librarian/Lecturer,
Pastoral Theology,
Episcopal Divinity School

BOZAK, Lillian C.
-53 Hempstead Ave.
Rockville Centre, NY 11570
-(516) 678-6997
-Roman Catholic
-History of Christian Thought
-PhD, Marquette Univ., 1972
-Thesis: Problem of Faith and
Reason in Alfred Loisy's Thought
-Women in Christian Thought
-Assoc. Prof.,
Molloy College

BOZEMAN, (Rev.) Jean
-Lutheran School of Theology
1100 E. 55th St.
Chicago, IL 60615
-Lutheran
-Education Ministry and Church
Administration

BOZEMAN, (cont.)
-M.Ed., Temple Univ., 1972
M.A.R.S., Univ. of Chicago
Divinity School, 1979
-Assoc. Prof., Dean of Students,
Lutheran School of Theology

BRAUDE, Ann
-320 Temple
New Haven, CT 06511
-(203) 624-8283
-History of Religions, American
Religious History
-PhD, Yale Univ., pending
-"Jewish Women in 19th Century
American" in A Documentary
History of Women in Religion
in 19th Century America,
R. Ruether and R. Keller, eds.,
forthcoming
-Religious Ideals and American
Social Institutions

Brenneman, Mary G.
-Fiddlehead Farm
Worchester, VT
-MA, Social Sciences, Univ. of
Chicago
-Anthropology, Myth, Ritual and
Symbol
-Asst. Prof.,
Johnson State College

BREUININ, Arlene Mazak
-783 Roble Ave., #3
Menlo Park, CA 94025
-(415) 325-0286
-History of Indian Religions,
Hinduism
-PhD, Univ. of Chicago, Dept. of
South Asian Languages and Liter-
ature, expected 1981
-Thesis: Sākta Tantric Mysticism
and Yoga
-Pt. Gopinath Kaviraj's Under-
standing of the Tantric Tradi-
tions; Kashmir Saivism and
Bengal Tantrism

BROOTEN, Bernadette Joan
-School of Theology at Claremont
Claremont, CA 91711
-(714) 626-3521
-Catholic
-New Testament, Hellenistic
Judaism, Women in the Early
Church
-PhD, Harvard Univ.,
1980
-Thesis: Women as Leaders in
Paul and the Ancient Synagogue
-Women in Ancient Judaism, Syna-
gogue, Archaeology, Marriage in
Ancient Judaism and Christianity
-Visiting Asst. Prof.,
Claremont Graduate School,
School of Theology at Claremont

BROWN, Karen McCarthy
-464 W. Broadway
New York, NY 10012
-(212) 477-4522
-Sociology of Religions,
Caribbean Religions
-PhD, Temple Univ., 1976
-Thesis: Doorways to Gine: A
Structural Analysis of Haitian
Religious Imagery
-Women, Religion and Social
Change, Structural Analysis
-Asst. Prof., Sociology of Religion,
Drew Graduate and Theo. School

BUCHWALD, Lynne S.
-2243 Wallace St.
Philadelphia, PA 19130
-(215) 235-4051; 563-9599
-Jewish
-Old Testament, Literary
Issues
-PhD, Univ. of Pennsylvania,
1981
-Thesis: Principles of Literary
Association in Biblical Liter-
ature
-"Eve and Origin of Evil in the
Bible and the Jewish Tradition"

BUCKLEY, Jorunn Jacobsen
 -421 Furnace Brook Pkwy.
 Quincy, MA 02170
 -(617) 471-1725
 -History of Religions, Dualism,
 Gnosticism, Myth/Ritual
 -PhD, Univ. of Chicago, 1978
 -Visiting Scholar,
 Episcopal Divinity School

BUCKLEY, Mary I.
 -77-23 166th St.
 Flushing, NY 11366
 -Catholic
 -Systematic Theology
 -ThD, Univ. of Münster, Germany,
 1969
 -Dissertation and articles on
 liberation and justice
 -Asst. Prof.,
 St. John's Univ., NYC

BURGESS, Faith E.
 -7301 Germantown Ave.
 Philadelphia, PA 19119
 -(215) 248-4616
 -Lutheran
 -Church History, History of
 Christian Thought, Church-
 State Relations
 -D.Phil., Univ. of Basel,
 Switzerland, 1968
 -Thesis: Understanding of the
 Relationship of Church and
 State According to John
 Courtney Murray
 -Women in the Church
 -Dean; Assoc. Prof.,
 Church History,
 Lutheran Theo. Sem.
 at Philadelphia

BUTLER, (Sr.) Sara
 -P.O. Box 759
 Mobile, AL 36601
 -Systematics, Church and
 Sacraments
 -PhD
 -Dir., Adult Education,
 Diocese of Mobile

C

CAHILL, Lisa Sowle
 -30 Quincy Rd.
 Chestnut Hill, MA 02167
 -(617) 964-1825
 -Roman Catholic
 -Theological and Medical Ethics
 -PhD, Univ. of Chicago, 1976
 -Thesis: Euthanasia: A Protes-
 tant and a Catholic View
 -Articles in the Journal of
 Religious Ethics, Religious
 Studies Review, Journal of Med-
 icine and Philosophy
 -Method in Theo. Ethics
 -Asst. Prof., Theology,
 Boston College

CAMPBELL, Laetitia A., OP
 -20 Irving Park
 Watertown, MA 02172
 -Roman Catholic
 -Pastoral Practical, Pastoral and
 Religious Formation
 -D.Min., Andover Newton Theo. Sem.,
 expected 1982
 -Pastoral Formation for Sacra-
 mental Ministry and the Or-
 dained Person
 -Assoc. Dir., Field Education,
 St. John's Sem.

CARDMAN, Francine Jo
 -80 Craigie St.
 Somerville, MA 02143
 -(617) 625-8240
 -Roman Catholic
 -Historical Theology, Patristics
 -PhD, Yale Univ., 1974
 -Thesis: Tertullian on the Resur-
 rection
 -History of Spirituality, Feminism
 and Christianity, Ecumenical
 Theology
 -Assoc. Prof., Historical Theology,
 Weston School of Theology

CARR, Anne
-1700 E. 56 St., #3604
Chicago, IL 60637
-(312) 684-2305
-Roman Catholic
-Contemporary Religious
Thought
-PhD, Univ. of Chicago, 1971
-The Theological Method of Karl
Rahner
-Women and Religion
-Assoc. Dean; Assoc. Prof.,
Theology, Divinity School,
Univ. of Chicago

CHAMBERS, Bessie
-48 Lake Ave., NE #2
Woburn, MA 01801
-(617) 933-7668
-Roman Catholic
-Psychology, Pastoral/Practical
-PhD, Boston College, 1963
-Thesis: An Experimental Study
between the need Counseling and
the Understanding of Love
-Correlation between Human/Divine
Relationships
-Prof., Pastoral Theology,
Episcopal Divinity School

CHRIST, Carol P.
-255 S. Cragmont Ave.
San Jose, CA 95127
-(408) 926-8321
-Religion and Culture, Contem-
porary Religious Thought, Women
and Religion, Symbolism
-PhD, Yale Univ., 1974
-Diving Deep and Surfacing:
Women Writers on Spiritual Quest
-Symbolism in Feminist Theology
and Spirituality
-Assoc. Prof.,
San Jose State Univ.

CLARK, Elizabeth A.
-1104 William St., #812
Fredericksburg, VA 22401
-(703) 373-1443

CLARK, Elizabeth A. (cont.)
-History of Christianity,
Patristics
-PhD, Columbia Univ., 1964
-Clement's Use of Aristotle: The
Aristotelian Contribution to
Clement of Alexandria's Refuta-
tion of Gnosticism; Women and
Religion: A Feminist Sourcebook
of Christian Thought; Jerome,
Chrysostom, and Friends
-Women in the Patristic Era
-Prof., Religion; Chair., Dept. of
Classics, Philosophy and Religion,
Mary Washington College

CLARK, Linda J.
-85 Jamaica St.
Jamaica Plain, MA 02130
-(617) 524-1407
-Music in the Church
-SMD, Union Theo. Sem., 1973
-Thesis: Music in Trinity Church,
Boston: 1890-1900
-Hymnody, Women and Worship
-Asst. Prof., Church Music,
Boston Univ.

CONGDON-MARTIN, (Rev.) Elizabeth W.
-72 Benefit St.
Attleboro, Ma 02703
-(617) 222-1440
-American Baptist
-Pastoral Practical Theology,
Education in Supervision
-M.Div., Colgate Rochester
Divinity School, 1974
-Use of Myers-Briggs Type Indi-
cator in field education rela-
tionship, Place of spiritual
guidance in the seminary curri-
culum
-Adjunct Faculty,
Church and Ministry Dept.,
Andover Newton Theo. School

COOEY-NICHOLS, Paula Martin
-132 Antrium St.
Cambridge, MA 02139
-(617) 491-7443

COOEY-NICHOLS, (cont.)
-Methodist
-Theology and Philosophy of Re-
ligion, Modern and Contemporary
Religious Thought
-PhD., Harvard Univ., 1981
-Thesis: Nature as Divine Self-
Communication in the Thought of
Jonathan Edwards: Toward a Con-
temporary Theology of Nature
-Women's Spirituality, Women and
Nature
-Research/Resources Assoc.,
Women's Studies in Religion,
Harvard Divinity School

COSSETTE, Ann D.
-1588 W. 42nd St.
Erie, PA 16509
-Contemporary Religious
Thought, Systematics
-PhD, Marquette Univ., 1973
-"Pan-Christic Vision of Maurice
Blondel"
-Development of Religious Thought
from Renaissance to Twentieth
Century
-Asst. Prof.,
Villa Maria College

COX, Patricia L.
-Dept. of Religion
Syracuse Univ.
Syracuse, NY 13210
-(315) 423-3861
-Episcopal
-History of Western Religions,
Graeco-Roman Studies
-PhD, Univ. of Chicago, 1979
-Thesis: Graeco-Roman Biographies
-Metaphor and Allegory in Anti-
quity
-Asst. Prof., Syracuse Univ.

CROKE, Prudence Mary, OSM
-Salve Regina College
Newport, RI 02840
-(401) 847-3137; 847-6650
-Roman Catholic

CROKE, (cont.)
-Contemporary Religious Thought,
Systematics and Sacramental
Theology, Religious Education
-PhD, Boston Univ., 1975
-Thesis: Roman Catholic Concepts
of the Eucharist and Spiritual
Growth in Interrelation with
Erikson's Theory of Development
in the Life Span
-Contemporary Spirituality
-Assoc. Prof., Religious Studies,
Salve Regina College

CROSTHWAITE, Jane F.
-Dept. of Religion
Mount Holyoke College
South Hadley, MA 01075
-Baptist
-History, Religion and Culture,
American Religious History
-PhD, Duke Univ., 1972
-Research on Emily Dickinson, Wo-
men in American Religious History
-Asst. Prof.,
Mount Holyoke College

CROTEAU-CHONKA, Clarisse D.
-3000 W. Grace St.,
Richmond, VA 23221
-(804) 358-3325
-Roman Catholic
-Religious Education, Practical
Theology
-PhD, Princeton Theo. Sem.,
expected 1981
-Thesis: Creative Intuition and
Religious Education
-Adult Faith Development, The-
ological Foundations of Christian
Education, Media and Christian
Education, and Ecumenical Mar-
iages and Their Impact on Chris-
tian Education
-Coordinator, Adult Education,
Diocese of Richmond, VA

CROUCH, Jacqueline, SM
   -25 W. 25th Ave., #4
   San Mateo, CA 94403
   -(415) 341-1554
   -Roman Catholic
   -Pastoral Theology, Adult
   Religious Education
   -D.Min., Jesuit School of The-
   ology, Berkeley, 1980
   -Theology, Scripture, Religious
   Studies, Liberation Theology
   for Middle America
   -Dir., Center for Religion, Edu-
   cation, and Society

CRUNKLETON, Martha
   -1116 S. Alfred St., #161-C
   Alexandria, VA 22314
   -(703) 836-6352
   -Philosophy of Religion
   -PhD, Vanderbilt Univ., 1981
   -Thesis: Language and Religion
   -Legislative Aide,
   Delegate Robert E. Washington,
   Virginia House of Delegates

CULP, Mildred L.
   -Seattle Univ.
   Seattle, WA 98122
   -(206) 626-5717
   -Religion and Culture, History
   of Culture
   -PhD, Univ. of Chicago, 1976
   -Religious Dimensions of Litera-
   ture and of Dance; American
   Jewish Literature
   -Asst. Prof., Seattle Univ.

CUNNINGHAM, (Sr.) Agnes, SSCM
   -St. Mary of the Lake Sem.
   Mundelein, IL 60510
   -(312) 566-6401
   -STD, Facultes Catholiques,
   Lyon, France, 1968
   -Assoc. Prof., Patrology and
   Historical Theology

CURTIS, (Rev.) Jean G.
   -424 Walnut St.
   Brookline, MA 02146
   -(617) 731-6772
   -United Church of Christ
   -Pastoral Practical,Parish
   Ministry, Urban
   -M.Div., Andover Newton Theo.
   School, 1979
   -Working Mothers; Here I Am,
   Take My Hand; A Parent's Guide
   to Nursery Schools
   -Asst. Minister,
   Old South Church, Boston;
   Visiting Lecturer,
   Andover Newton Theo. School

DARLING, Robin
   -5305 Wehawken Rd.
   Glen Echo, MD 20016
   -(301) 229-2820
   -History of Religion, History of
   Christianity, Ancient Syrian
   Christianity
   -PhD, Univ. of Chicago, 1980
   -Thesis: The Patriarchate of
   Severus of Antioch
   -Early Christian Asceticism
   -Instr., History of Christianity,
   Wesley Theo. Sem.

DAVANEY, Sheila Greeve
   -Iliff School of Theology
   Denver, CO   80210
   -(303) 744-1287
   -Philosophy of Religion, Con-
   temporary Theology, Women's
   Studies
   -ThD, Harvard Univ., 1980
   -Thesis: The Idea of Divine
   Power in the Thought of Karl
   Barth and Charles Hartshorne:
   Foundations and Implications
   -Feminism and Process Thought

DAVIS, Dena S.
-School of Religion
Gilman Hall
Univ. of Iowa
Iowa City, IA 52240
-Ethics, Biomedical Ethics
-PhD, Univ. of Iowa, expected
1982
-Autonomy, Informed Consent
-Teaching Asst., Univ. of Iowa

DECONCINI, Barbara
-475 Cherokee Ave., SE
Atlanta, GA 30312
-(404) 523-4400
-Religion and Culture, 20th Cen-
tury Literature, Phenomenology,
Hermeneutics, Liturgical and
Ritual Studies
-PhD, Emory Univ., 1980
-Thesis: Memory, Time, and Iden-
tity: A Hermeneutical Inquiry
-Chair., Academic Studies Dept.,
Atlanta College of Art

DELEEUW, Patricia E.
-Dept. of Theology
Boston College
Chestnut Hill, MA 02167
-(617) 969-0100 x3894
-History of Christian Thought
-PhD, Univ. of Toronto, 1979
-"The Village Parish in the
Early Middle Ages" in The
Medieval Village, ed., J.A.
Raftis
-Asst. Prof., Boston College

DILLENBERGER, Jane
-80 Sherman St.
Hartford, CT 06105
-(203) 232-9232
-Episcopal
-Religion and the Visual Arts,
American Religious Art and
Architecture
-MA, Radcliffe College, 1944
-Extensive Publications
-Adjunct Faculty,
Hartford Sem. Foundation

DIMMITT, Cornelia
-Theology Dept.
Georgetown Univ.
Washington, DC 20057
-(202) 625-4874
-History of Religions
-PhD, Syracuse Univ., 1970
-Assoc. Prof., Georgetown Univ.

DOHERTY, Anne
-3 Phillips Place
Cambridge, MA 02138
-(617) 492-1960
-Roman Catholic
-Psychology and Religion,
Clinical Psychology
-PhD, Catholic Univ. of America,
1969
-Journal of Experimental Psychol-
ogy, Developmental Psychology,
Religious Life in the 70s
-Women in Church Administration
and Ministry, Gender and Minis-
try, Moral Development of Women
-Assoc. Prof., Pastoral Psychology,
Weston School of Theology

DOOLEY, Anne Mary, SSJ
-Niagara Univ.
Niagara University, NY 14109
-(716) 285-1212 x251
-Roman Catholic
-Psychology and Religion, Con-
temporary Religious Thought,
Business
-D.Min., Colgate Rochester/
Bexley Hall/Crozer Theo. Sem.,
1979
-"Pastoral Counseling and the Ob-
sessive-Compulsive Personality
in Quest of Religious Maturity"
-Religious Development in Early
Childhood, Women in Church and
Society, Christian Communities
and Communes
-Asst. Prof.,
Religious Studies.
Niagara Univ.

DOUGLASS, Jane Dempsey
-School of Theology at Claremont
 W. Foothill Blvd. at College Ave.
 Claremont, CA 91711
-(714) 626-3521
-United Presbyterian Church, U.S.A.
-History of Christian Thought,
 Philosophy of Religion
-PhD, Harvard Univ., 1963
-Justification in Late Medieval
 Preaching: A Study of John
 Geiler of Keiserberg; "Women
 and the Continental Reformation"
 in Religion and Sexism: Images
 of Woman in the Jewish and Chris-
 tian Traditions, R. Reuther, ed.
-Prof., Church History,
 School of Theology at Claremont ;
 Prof., Religion,
 Claremont Graduate School

DOWNING, Chris
-625 Serpentine
 Del Mar, CA 92014
-(714) 481-0685; 265-5185
-Religion and Culture
-PhD, Drew Univ., 1966
-Freud, Jung, Classical Myth-
 ology, Goddess Traditions
-Prof.; Chair.,
 San Diego State Univ.

DREYER, Elizabeth
-4141 Martin Dr.
 Milwaukee, WI 53208
-(414) 933-6689
-Roman Catholic
-Theology
-PhD, Marquette Univ., 1981
-Thesis: Affectus in
 Bonaventure's Description of
 the Journey of the Soul to God
-Teaching Asst., Marquette Univ.

DUMAIS, Monique
-39 St. Jean-Baptiste Ouesar
 Rimouski, P. Quebec
 Canada, G5L 4J2

DUMAIS, (cont.)
-Ethics
-Prof.,
 Univ. du Quebec, Rimouski

DUNN, Rose Ellen
-Box 498
 Drew Univ.
 Madison, NJ 07940
-(201) 966-0234
-Philosophy of Religion
-PhD, Drew Univ. Graduate School,
 pending

EARLEY, Margaret
-3401 S. 39th St.
 Milwaukee, WI 53215
-(414) 671-5400
-Roman Catholic
-Contemporary Religious Thought,
 Historical and Systematic The-
 ology
-PhD, Marquette Univ., 1973
-Thesis: H. Richard Niebuhr's
 Theory of Revelation
-Sacramental Theology
-Prof., Religious Studies,
 Alverno College

EDELMAN, Alice Chasan
-224 B Marshall Street
 Princeton, NJ 08540
-(609) 921-7673
-Methodological Studies: Modern
 Jewish Social and Intellectual
 History
-PhD, Univ. of Pennsylvania, 1977
-Thesis: Critical Analysis of
 Theories of Secularization and
 Their Applicability to Modern
 Jewish History
-Asst. Dir.,
 B'nai Brith Hillel Foundation,
 Princeton Univ.

EDWARDS, (Rev.) Sarah A.
-63 Bayberry Hill Rd.
 Avon, CT 06001
-(203) 677-4235
-United Church of Christ
-Biblical Studies, New Testament
-PhD, Hartford Sem. Foundation,
 1974
-Thesis: P75 and B in the Fourth
 Gospel: A Study of the History
 of the Text
-P75 Under the Magnifying Glass,
 in Novum Testamentum; co-editor
 of Festschrift on Christological
 Perspectives; Women in Biblical/
 Theo. Perspective
-Adjunct Prof., Biblical Studies,
 Hartford Sem. Foundation

ELWELL, Ellen Sue Levi
-416 Eastside Dr.
 Bloomington, IN 47401
-(219) 332-6514; 337-7086
-Jewish
-Judaica, Religious Education,
 Adult Education, Jewish Women
-PhD, Indiana Univ., 1980
-History of National Council of
 Jewish Women, Jewish Women in
 Organizations, esp. Sociology
 of German Jewish Immigrants,
 and (informal) Jewish Education
 of Women Throughout History
-Asst. Dir., Religious Studies
 Project, Indiana Univ.

EXUM, J. Cheryl
-Dept. of Theology
 Boston College
 Chestnut Hill, MA 02167
-(617) 969-0100 x3880
-Old Testament, Literary An-
 alysis of Biblical Texts
-PhD, Columbia Univ., 1976
-Asst. Prof., Old Testament,
 Boston College

FALK, Nancy Ellen Auer
-4101 Katydid Lane
 Kalamazoo, MI 49008
-(616) 375-9745; 383-2326
-History of (South Asian)
 Religions
-PhD, Univ. of Chicago, 1972
-Unspoken Worlds: Women's Reli-
 gious Lives in Non-Western Cul-
 tures (with R. Gross); Women's
 Religious Roles and Lives,
 Cross-Cultural
-Prof., Western Michigan Univ.

FALLS, Helen E.
-3939 Gentilly Blvd.
 New Orleans, LA 70126
-EdD, D.D. (Hon.)
-Prof. of Missions,
 New Orleans Baptist Theo. Sem.

FELDHAUS, Anne
-129 W. 75th St.
 New York, NY 10023
-(212) 724-6591
-History of Religions, Medieval
 and Popular Hinduism
-PhD, Univ. of Pennsylvania, 1976
-Thesis: Old Marathi Literature
 of Mahanubhava Sect
-Medieval Indian Biography and
 Autobiography, Pilgrimage Cen-
 ters in Maharashtra
-Asst. Prof., Theology,
 Fordham Univ.

FINALY, Ellison Banks
-120 Bishop St.
 New Haven, CT 06511
-PhD
-History of Religions (Hinduism/
 Indian Buddhism)
-Instr., Mt. Holyoke College
 South Hadley, MA

FIORENZA, Elisabeth Schüssler
-Dept. of Theology
Notre Dame Univ.
Notre Dame, IN 46556
-(219) 232-1523
-Catholic
-New Testament Studies and Pastoral Theology
-Dr. Theol., Univ. of Münster, 1970
-Revelation and Women in Early Christianity
-Extensive Publications
-Assoc. Prof., Theology, Univ. of Notre Dame

FISCHER, Clare B.
-3025 Fulton St.
Berkeley, CA 94705
-(415) 845-8312
-Religion and Culture, Theology of Work
-PhD, Graduate Theo. Union, Berkeley, 1979
-Thesis: The Fiery Bridge: Simone Weil's Theology of Work
-Women, Work, and Vocation
-Adjunct Faculty, San Francisco Theo. Sem.

FISHBURN, Janet F.
-1694 Princeton Dr.
State College, PA 16801
-PhD, Penn State Univ.
-American Religious Studies

FOLEY, M. Nadine, OP
-1257 E. Siena Heights Dr.
Adrian, MI 49221
-(517) 265-5135
-Roman Catholic
-Contemporary Religious Thought, Scripture and Philosophy
-PhD, Catholic Univ. of America, 1956; S.T.M., Union Theo. Sem., NYC, 1971
-Articles on Women in the Roman Catholic Church
-Vicaress, Adrian Dominican Sisters

FOLLIS, Elaine R.
-Principia College
Elsah, IL 62028
-(618) 374-2131
-Christian Science
-Old Testament, History and Language
-PhD, Boston Univ., 1976
-Thesis: The Sea in the Poetry of Israel, Ugarit, Greece, and Rome
-Helleno-Semitic Studies, History of Israel
-Assoc. Prof., Principia College

FONTAINE, Carole R.
-99 Herrick Circle
Newton Centre, MA 02159
-(617) 964-6542
-Episcopal
-Old Testament, Wisdom Literature, Middle Eygptian, History of Religions, Islam
-PhD, Duke Univ., 1979
-Thesis: The use of the Traditional Saying in the Old Testament
-Folklorist, Methodologies, Structural Anthropology, Liberation Theology, High Energy Physics
-Asst. Prof., Andover Newton Theo. School

FOSTER, Leila M.
-1585 Ridge Ave.
Evanston, IL 60201
-(312) 666-6500 x489; 328-8562
-United Methodist
-Psychology of Religion, Law/Ministry/Psychology
-JD, Northwestern Univ., 1953
-PhD, Northwestern Univ., 1966
-Thesis: Theological Implications of Ego Identity
-Adjunct Assoc. Prof., Psychology, Univ. of Illinois Medical Ctr., Chicago

FURMAN, Frida Kerner
-2341 Echo Park Ave.
Los Angeles, CA 90026
-(213) 661-8290
-Ethics, Sociology of Religion
-PhD, Univ. of Southern California
-Thesis: The Construction of American Jewish Identity: A Case Study
-Contemporary Religious Consciousness and Identity in America, Women in Religion
-Instr.,
Univ. of Southern California

GAVENTA, Beverly Roberts
-1100 S. Goodman
Rochester, NY 14620
-(716) 271-1320
-New Testament, Pauline Studies
-PhD, Duke Univ., 1978
-Thesis: Paul's Conversion: A Critical Sifting of the Epistolary Evidence
-Assoc. Prof.,
Colgate Rochester Divinity School

GETZ, Lorine M.
-61 Grove St.
Somerville, MA 02144
-(617) 969-2946
-Religion and Literature, Religion and Culture, Contemporary Religious Thought, Women and Religion
-PhD, Univ. of St. Michael's College, Toronto, 1979
-Thesis: Types of Grace in Flannery O'Connor's Fiction
-Flannery O'Connor: Her Life, Library and Book Reviews; Bergman's Films, Women's Spirituality, Jungian Psychology
-Exec. Coordinator,
Boston Theo. Institute

GLEASON, M. Elizabeth, CSJ
-Aquinas Jr. College
15 Walnut Park
Newton, MA 02158
-(617) 244-8134

GOING, Cathleen M.
-Thomas More Institute
3421 Drummond St.
Montreal, Quebec, CANADA H3G 1X7
-Contemporary Religious Thought, Work of Aquinas
-PhD, St. Mary's Graduate School of Theology, 1956
-Co-editor, The Question as Commitment; Work of B. Lonergan, Research in Adult-Learning Theory
-Pres.; Lecturer,
Thomas More Institute

GOLDENBERG, Naomi R.
-Univ. of Ottawa
Dept. of Religious Studies
177 Waller Street
Ottawa, Ontario, CANADA K1N 6N5
-(613) 231-2300
-Psychology and Religion
-PhD, Yale Univ., 1976
-Changing of the Gods: Feminism and the End of Traditional Religion; Psychoanalysis and Cognitive Systems
-Asst. Prof., Univ. of Ottawa

GOOSEN, Marilyn M.
-Dijk 13 A
6644 KB Ewijk
The Netherlands
-08872-1583
-Roman Catholic
-Contemporary Religious Thought, Christian Mysticism, Spirituality
-S.T.D., Univ. of Nijmege, 1977
-Christian Mysticism: Transcending Techniques

GORMAN, Margaret
  -Boston College
  Chestnut Hill, MA   02167
  -(617) 969-0100 x3844
  -Ethics and Religious Education,
  Psychology
  -PhD, Catholic Univ. of America,
  1956
  -Semantics, Thomism

GREELEY, Dolores, RSM
  -2039 N. Geyer Rd.
  St. Louis, MO   63131
  -PhD
  -Systematic/Historical Theology
  -Asst. Prof.,
  Dept. of Theo. Studies;
  Dir. of Undergraduates Studies,
  St. Louis Univ.

GRIFFIN, (Sr.) Isabel Mary
  -Immaculata College
  Immaculata, PA   19345
  -MA, Dogmatic Theology
  -Asst. Prof., Chair.,
  Religious Studies Dept.,
  Immaculata College

GROSS, Rita M.
  -Dept. of Philosophy and
  Religious Studies
  Eau Claire, WI   54701
  -History of Religions, Women and
  Religions, India, Preliterates
  -PhD, Univ. of Chicago, 1975
  -Unspoken Worlds: Women's Reli-
  gious Lives in Non-Western Cul-
  tures (with N.E.A. Falk); Bud-
  dhism, Goddess Religions

GUDORF, Christine E.
  -Xavier Univ.
  Cincinnati, OH   45207
  -(513) 242-6380
  -Roman Catholic
  -Ethics, Liberation Theology
  -PhD, Columbia/Union Theo. Sem.,
  -Catholic Social Teaching on
  Liberation, Economic Justice
  -Asst. Prof., Dept. of Theology
  Xavier Univ.

HADDAD, Yvonne Yazbeck
  -77 Sherman St.
  Hartford, CT   06150
  -(203) 232-4451
  -History of Religions, Islam in
  the Twentieth Century
  -PhD, Hartford Sem. Foundation,
  1980
  -Thesis: The Significance of the
  Concept of History in Modern
  Islam
  -The Islamic Understanding of
  Death and Resurrection; Contem-
  porary Muslim Understanding of
  the Qur'an; Sexuality, Female
  Roles, and Liberation in Islam,
  Muslims in North America
  -Assoc. Prof., Islamic Studies,
  Hartford Sem. Foundation

HAMMETT, Jenny Y.
  -Box 64
  Wells College
  Aurora, NY   13026
  -(315) 364-8748
  -Contemporary Religious Thought,
  Psychology and Religion, Phi-
  losophy of Religion
  -PhD, Syracuse Univ., 1973
  -Transformations of Conscious-
  ness: Theology as Woman's Quest,
  forthcoming; Articles in
  Sounding, Religion in Life,
  Anima, Journal of Pastoral
  Counseling; Relationship between
  Women's Models of Consciousness
  and Brain Hemispheres
  -Asst. Prof., Religion and
  Philosophy, Wells College

HARRINGTON, Patricia A.
  -5254 S. Dorchester, #212
  Chicago, IL   60615
  -(312) 241-5047

HARRINGTON, (cont.)
-Contemporary Religious Thought
-PhD, Univ. of Chicago, expected
1981
-Thesis: Mary: Conflicting Models
in Interpretation of Religious
Symbol
-Psychology of Religion, Feminist
Theology, Hermeneutics

HARRIS, E. Lynn
-P.O. Box 412
Wheaton, IL 60187
-(312) 393-1034
-New Testament, Old Testament,
Religion and Literature, Reli-
gious Education, Religion and
Public Education
-D. Min., Chicago Theo. Sem.,
1978; PhD, New York Univ., 1980
-Thesis: The Thought of Aidan
Wilson Tozer: An Analysis and
Appraisal with Special Emphasis
on His Mysticism and Conceptual
Approach to the World
-Methods of Teaching Bible at a
state-supported University,
Mystic Spirituality, Women and
Religion; Poetry and Reviews
-Asst. Prof.,
Univ. of Illinois, Chicago Circle

HARRIS, Maria
-216 St. Paul St.
Brookline, MA 02146
-(617) 277-9710
-Roman Catholic
-Religious Education, Pastoral
Theology
-EdD, Columbia/Union Theo. Sem.,
1971
-Thesis: The Aesthetic Dimension
of Religious Education
-Portrait of Ministry, DRE Reader,
Parish Religious Education, DRE
Book, Experiences in Community
-Assoc. Prof., Religious Education
Andover Newton Theo. School

HARRIS, Rivkah
-6114 N. Washtenaw
Chicago, IL 60659
-Ancient Near Eastern Religion
-PhD,
-Assoc. Prof., Northwestern Univ.

HAYDOCK, Ann S.
-1911 Spruce Hill Rd.
Pickering, Ontario
CANADA L1V I5G
-(416) 839-4815
-Psychology and Religion, Con-
temporary Religious Thought,
Sexist Linguistics, Women in
Religious Thought
-BA, Goddard College, 1979
-"The Beginning, the Word, and
the Goddess: The Reappropriation
of Feminine Power"

HAYWOOD, Carol Lois
-880 Chestnut St.
Waban, MA 02168
-(617) 969-6049
-Assoc. of Evan. Lutheran Churches
-Sociology of Religion, Women in
Cults, Working Class Religion
-PhD, Boston Univ., pending

HEYWARD, I. Carter
-101 Brattle St.
Cambridge, MA 02138
-(617) 868-3450
-Episcopal
-Systematic Theology, Contem-
porary/Liberation and Feminist
Theology
-PhD, Union Theo. Sem., 1980
-Thesis: The Redemption of God:
A Theology of Mutual Relation
-A Priest Forever; Sexuality,
Women's Studies, Latin American
Theology
-Asst. Prof., Theology,
Episcopal Divinity School

HIATT, (Rev.) Suzanne R.
-99 Brattle St.
Cambridge, MA 02138
-(617) 868-3450
-Episcopal
-Pastoral Theology, Urban Theology, Crisis Counseling, Sociology of Religion
-M.Div., Episcopal Divinity School, 1964; M.S.W., Boston Univ., 1965
-Co-author, Women Priests: Yes or No?; History of Women in the American Episcopal Church, Experience of Women Clergy
-Prof., Pastoral Theology, Episcopal Divinity School

HOLLER, Linda
-3203 Overlook Dr.
Nashville, TN 37212
-(615) 297-2860
-Ethics, Phenomenology
-PhD, Vanderbilt Univ., 1980
-Thesis: Relation of Consciousness and Life-World to Moral Discernment
-Phenomenological Description of Moral Agency

HOSTETLER, Beulah S.
-2550 Ball Rd.
Willow Grove, PA 19090
-(215) 659-4894
-Mennonite
-Religion and Culture, Religion in America
-PhD, Univ. of Pennsylvania, 1977
-Thesis: Franconia Mennonite Conference and American Protestant Movements 1840-1940

HOWE, E. Margaret
-Dept. of Philosophy and Religion
Western Kentucky Univ.
Bowling Green, KY 42101
-(502) 745-3136
-New Testament and Patristics, Biblical History and Literature
-PhD, Univ. of Manchester, England, 1964
-Women and Church Leadership, Celibacy and Priesthood, Women in Patristic Literature; "Interpretations of Paul in the Acts of Paul and Thecla"
-Assoc. Prof., Western Kentucky Univ.

HOWELL, Maribeth
-1224 E. Northern
Phoenix, AZ 85020
-(602) 997-7397
-Catholic
-Old Testament
-S.T.L., St. Paul Univ., 1979
-Psalm Study, Structural Analysis
-Instr., Kino Institute

HUNT, Mary E.
-Isedet Camacua 282
1406 Buenos Aires
ARGENTINA
-Contemporary Religious Thought
-PhD, Graduate Theo. Union, 1980
-Thesis: Feminist Liberation Theology: The Development of Method in Construction
-Dept. of Theology, Instituto Superior Evangelico de Estudios Teologicos

I

IDZIAK, Janine Marie
- Dept. of Philosophy and Religion
  Wallace 202
  Eastern Kentucky Univ.
  Richmond, KY 40475
- (606) 623-6C82
- History of Christian Thought,
  Ethics, Philosophy of Religion,
  Medieval Period
- PhD, Univ. of Michigan, 1975
- Divine Command Morality:
  Historical and Contemporary
  Readings
- Dept. of Philosophy and Religion,
  Eastern Kentucky Univ.

J

JANCOSKI, Loretta
- 15400 Carriage Lane
  Mishawaka, IN 46544
- Religion and Psychology
- Phd
- Adjunct Asst. Prof.,
  Pastoral Theology,
  Univ. of Notre Dame

JAY, Nancy B.
- 6 Walley St.
  Bristol, RI 0280C
- (401) 253-9533
- Sociology, Sociology of Religion
- PhD, Brandeis, 1981
- Thesis: A General Sociology
  of Blood Sacrifice
- "Gender and Dichotomy"
- Research Resources Assoc.,
  Harvard Divinity School

JONTE, Diane E.
- 4100 Campana Dr.
  Palo Alto, CA 94396
- (415) 494-2944
- Psychology of Religion,
  Religion and the Social
  Sciences, Women and Religion
- PhD, Univ. of Chicago, 1980
- Thesis: Religion and Psychology
  in the Thought of Hermann
  Rorschach
- "Ego Functions in a Variety of
  Dream States"; Gnosticism
- Instr., p.t., Holy Names College
  and John F. Kennedy Univ.

JUNG, Patricia B.
- 224 Seventh Ave., S.
  Moorhead, MN 56560
- (218) 236-5907
- Theological Ethics
- PhD, Vanderbilt Univ., 1979
- Thesis: Human Embodiment and
  Moral Character: A Revision of
  Stanley Hauerwas in Light of
  Paul Ricouer's Philosophy of
  the Will
- "The Moral Dimension of Life-
  style" in Lifestyle: Theory,
  Practice, and Research, Baruch
  and Eckstein, eds.
- Asst. Prof., Concordia College

K

KARWEDSKY, Linda Schleicher
- 765 McMurray Dr. #0-14
  Nashville, TN 37211
- (615) 331-2742; 322-4843
- History of Christian Thought,
  Feminist Theology
- MA, Florida State Univ., 1979
- Staff Asst., Women's Center,
  Vanderbilt Univ.

KEARNEY, Suzanne M., CSJ
-558 South Ave.
 Weston, MA 02193
-(617) 899-5500
-New Testament Studies
-PhD, Boston Univ., 1977
-Thesis: Principal Composi-
 tional Techniques in Luke-Acts;
 Parables, Synoptics
-Prof., Pope John XXIII Univ.

KEHOE, Nancy Clare, RSCJ
-112 Appleton St.
 Boston, MA 02116
-(617) 492-6989
-Roman Catholic
-Psychology and Spiritual Di-
 rection, Therapy
-PhD, Boston College, 1974
-Thesis: Study of Nonverbal Com-
 munications and the Effect Coun-
 seling Training Has on the
 Ability to Read Nonverbal Cues
-Mental Health Systems and
 Clergy, Community Agencies and
 the Need to Work Together
-Dept. of Psychiatry,
 Cambridge Hospital;
 Visiting Lecturer,
 Episcopal Divinity School

KELLER, Rosemary Skinner
-2725 Mohawk Ave.
 Woodridge, IL 60515
-(312) 968-4868
-United Methodist
-Ethics, Religion and Culture,
 American Church History, Women
 in American Church History
-PhD, Univ. of Illinois at
 Chicago Circle, 1977
-American Women and Religion:
 The 19th Century: A Documentary
 History, with Rosemary ruether
-Asst. Prof.,
 Garrett Evan. Theo. Sem.

KILLEN, Patricia O'Connell
-Univ. of the South
 Sewanee, TN 37375
-(615) 598-5931 x378

KILLEN, (cont.)
-Catholic
-History of Religions, American
 Religion and Society
-PhD, Stanford Univ., pending
-Thesis: The Machine in the
 Kingdom of God: The Place of
 Technology in a Holy Community

KING, Sallie B.
-606 Longmeadow Rd.
 Amherst, NY 14226
-(716) 832-6164
-History of Religions, Philosophy
 of Religion, Chinese Buddhism,
 Comparative Philosophy of
 Religion
-PhD, Temple Univ., 1980
-Thesis: the Active Self in
 Tathāgatagarbha-Buddha Nature
 Thought, Buddha Nature Treatise
-Lect., State Univ. College,
 Buffalo

KINSCHNER, Julia
-Graduate Dept. of Religion
 Vanderbilt Univ.
 Nashville, TN 37240
-(615) 322-4833
-Contemporary Religious Thought,
 Systematics, Jungian Psychology,
 Phenomenology
-Asst. to Director,
 Vanderbilt Univ. Women's Center

KLUEPFEL, Marie Patricia McIntyre
-P.O. Box 180
 West Mystic, CT 06388
-MA, Marquette Univ., 1965
-Editor, Religion Teacher's
 Journal

KOEHLER, Joan SSSF
-1527 S. 24th St.
 Milwaukee, WI 53204
-MA, Scripture
-Asst. Prof., Religious Studies,
 Alverno College

KOLLER-FOX, Cherie
-41 Locke St.
Cambridge, MA 02140
-EdD, Harvard Graduate School
of Education, pending
-Learning Environments, Jewish
Education

KRAEMER, Ross S.
-2419 Pine St.
Philadelphia, PA 19103
-(215) 732-9333
-Jewish
-History of Religions in the
Greco-Roman World
-PhD, Princeton Univ., 1976
-"Ecstasy and Possession:
Women in the Cult of Dionysus";
Goddesses and Women's Roles in
the Greco-Roman World
-Asst. to the President,
Stockton State College,
Pomona, NJ

KROEGER, Catherine Clark
-19 Kenwood Parkway
St. Paul, MN 55105
-(612) 277-4505
-New Testament and Classics
-MA, Univ. of Minnesota, 1980
-Women in Ancient Religion,
St. Paul on Women
-Teaching Assoc.,
Univ. of Minnesota

KUJAWA, Sheryl A.
-37 Mt. Vernon St.
Cambridge, MA 02140
-(617) 492-7077
-Roman Catholic
-Church History, Women's History,
American Religious History
-MTS, Harvard Divinity School,
1981
-Articles/Bibliographies in Fem-
inist Publications
-Archival Asst.,
Schlesinger Library on the
History of Women in America

L

LAFFEY, Alice L.
-3333 Fifth Ave.
Latrobe, PA 15650
-(412) 578-6256
··Roman Catholic
-Old Testament, Historical
Books
-S.S.D., Pontifical Biblical In-
stitute, expected 1981
-Thesis: The Literary Function
of the Prophecy of Nathan in
the Deuteronomic History
-OT Symbolic Language
-Faculty, St. Vincent Sem.

LANDES, Paula Frederiksen
-Dept. of Religious Studies
Stanford Univ.
-(415) 497-3322
-History of Religions, Early
Christianity, Late Antiquity
-PhD, Princeton Univ., 1979
-Thesis: Augustine's Early Inter-
pretation of Paul
-"Augustine and His Analysts,"
"Hysteria and the Gnostic Myths
of Creation"
-Pauline Letters, Augustine's
Theology of Sexuality
-Mellon Fellow, Stanford Univ.

LEAMING, (Rev.) Marjorie Newlin
-438 View Dr.
Santa Paula, CA 93060
-(805) 525-8859
-Unitarian Universalist
-BD, Meadville Lombard Theo.
School, 1967
-Feminism from the Pulpit
-Feminist Theology
-Sr. Minister.,
Unitarian Universalist Church,
Santa Paula, CA

LEBACQZ, Karen
-Pacific School of Religion
Berkeley, CA 94709
-(415) 848-0528
-United Church of Christ
-Ethics, Bioethics
-PhD, Harvard Univ., 1974
-Essays in Bioethics
-Assoc. Prof.,
Pacific School of Religion

LEWIS, Eleanor V.
-4102 Colonial Rd.
Pikesville, MD   21218
-(301) 323-3200; 486-3840
-Roman Catholic
-History of Christian Thought,
Late Medieval and Reformation
-PhD, Fordham Univ., 1970
-Thesis: Concepts of the Church
at the First Period of the
Council of Trent
-Women in the Church, Ecumenism
-Assoc. Prof., History and
Systematic Theology,
St. Mary Sem. and Univ.,
Baltimore, MD

LINDLEY, Susan Hill
-313 E. 6th St.
Northfield, MN 55057
-(507) 663-3094
-Episcopal
-History of Christian Thought,
American Religion
-PhD, Duke Univ., 1974
-Thesis: Catherine Beecher
-Asst. Prof., St. Olaf College

LIVEZEY, Lois Gehr
-7245 S. Merrill Ave.
Chicago, IL 60649
-Theology
-PhD, Univ. of Chicago Divinity
School, pending

LUMMIS, Adair T.
-77 Sherman St.
Hartford, CT 06150
-(203) 232-4451
-Sociology of Religion
-PhD, Columbia Univ., 1979
-Thesis: Especially Union?
(A study of how external situa-
tions and changes in higher ed-
ucation and organized religion
affected the internal dynamics
of a seminary.)
-Study of Clergywomen in Protes-
tant Church (1983)
-Research Assoc.,
Hartford Sem. Foundation

LUND, Shirley
-216 St. Paul St.
Brookline, MA 02146
-(617) 738-5133
-New Testament, Early Christian-
ity, Gospels, Tarqumim to the
Pentateuch
-PhD, Univ. of St. Andrews,
Scotland, 1967
-Thesis: Character of Marginal
Readings to Codex Neofih 1
-Assoc. Prof., Boston Univ.

LUNZ, ELISABETH
-341 Ponce de Leon Ave., NE
Atlanta, GA 30308
-(404) 873-1531
-Presbyterian
-Religion and Culture
-PhD, Tulane Univ., 1969
-The Grimke Sisters, Articles on
Theology and Literature
-Staff Assoc., Office of Women,
Presbyterian Centre

M

MALBON, Elizabeth Struthers
-Dept. of Philosophy and Religion,
Virginia Polytechnic Institute
and State Univ.
Blackburg, VA 24061
-(703) 961-5118
-New Testament, Humanities,
Mark, Structuralism
-PhD, Florida State Univ., 1980
-Semeia 17 (1979): 97-132
-Gospel of Mark, Structural
Exegesis
-Asst. Prof., Virginia Poly-
technic and State Univ.

MALLORY, Marilyn May
-Dijk 13 A
6644 KB Ewijk
The Netherlands
-08872-1583 (Holland)
-Roman Catholic
-Contemporary Religious Thought,
Christian Mysticism, Spiritu-
ality
-S.T.D., Univ. of Nijmegen, 1977
-Christian Mysticism: Tran-
scending Techniques

MARKS, Patricia Lynne
-80A Maple Ave.
Morristown, NJ 07960
-(201) 539-4361
-Roman Catholic
-Religious Education, Religion
and Psychology
-PhD, Drew Univ., pending
-Articles, Woman's Consciousness
-Director, Religious Education,
Assumption Church

MATTER, E. Ann
-Dept. of Religious Studies
Univ. of Pennsylvania
Philadelphia, PA 19104

MATTER, (cont.)
-(215) 243-8614
-Roman Catholic
-History of Christian Thought,
Medieval Christianity
-PhD, Yale Univ., 1976
-"De Parto Virgini": of Paschasius
Radbertus on Corpus Christianorum
-Articles., Carolingian Exegesis
-Asst. Prof.,
Univ. of Pennsylvania

MAURER, M. Sylvia, CSC
-St. Mary's College
Winona, MN 55987
-(502) 452-2993 x220
-Catholic
-Old and New Testament
-PhD, St. Mary's College, Notre
Dame, IN, 1967
-Prudence, Spirituality, Scrip-
ture and Literature

McCANDLESS, Bardarah
-Westminster College
New Wilmington, PA 16142
-(412) 946-8761
-United Presbyterian, U.S.A.
-Religious Education
-PhD, Univ. of Pittsburgh, 1968
-Religion and Personality Char-
acteristics, Psychology
-Assoc. Prof., Religion,
Westminster College

McCOLLUM, Adele Brannon
-Dept. of Philosophy and Religion
Montclair State College
Upper Montclair, NJ 07043
-(201) 893-5144
-Religion and Culture, Women's
Studies, Psychology of Carl Jung
-PhD, Syracuse Univ., 1972
-Thesis: Gerard Winstanley and
Myth in 17th Century Sectari-
anism
-Assoc. Prof., Philosophy and
Religion, Montclair State College

McDONOUGH, Marie Mahnken
  -3235 Steiner St.
   San Francisco, CA 94123
  -(415) 922-5138
  -History of Religions, Primitive
   Religions, Women and Religion
  -MA, St. Xavier College,
   Chicago, 1967
  -History of Women and Religion
   From Pre-History to Present,
   forthcoming; Women in Pre-
   History
  -Lecturer in Women and Religion,
   California

McDONOUGH, Sheila
  -Dept. of Religion
   Concordia Univ.
   Montreal, PQ CANADA
  -(514) 879-8521
  -Islamics
  -PhD, McGill Univ., 1963
  -Islamic Modernism, Women in
   Indian and Pakistani Islam
  -Prof., Concordia Univ.

McGINTY, Mary Peter, CSJ
  -Loyola Univ. of Chicago
   Chicago, IL 60626
  -(312) 274-3000
  -Roman Catholic
  -Contemporary Religious Thought,
   History of Christian Thought,
   Sacramental Theology
  -PhD, Marquette Univ., 1967
  -Thesis: Berengarius' Notion of
   Real Presence
  -Sacramental Life, Rahner, Pro-
   cess Thought
  -Asst. Prof., Theology; Director,
   Graduate Theology Program,
   Loyola-Chicago

McHATTEN, Mary Timothy, OP
  -Kino Institute
   1224 E. Northern Ave.
   Phoenix, AZ 85020
  -(602) 997-7397

McHATTEN, (cont.)
  -Catholic
  -Old Testament, Prophets
  -PhD, Univ. of Ottawa, 1979
  -Thesis: The Day of Yahweh: A
   Study of the Concept yôm Yahweh
   in the Old Testament
  -Apocalyptic Literature
  -Teaching-Prof., Kino Institute/
   Univ. of San Francisco

McWILLIAM-DEWART, Joanne
  -St. Michael's College
   Univ. of Toronto
   Toronto, Ont., M5S 1J4 CANADA
  -(416) 921-3151
  -History of Christian Thought,
   Patristics
  -PhD, Univ. of St. Michael's
   College, 1968
  -Theology of Grace of Theodore
   of Mopsuestia; Christology of
   Augustine
  -Assoc. Prof.,
   St. Michael's College

MEADOW, Mary Jo
  -1204 Highland Ave.
   Mankato, MN 56001
  -(507) 387-4276
  -Psychology and Religion
  -PhD, Univ. of Minnesota, 1976
  -Women and Religion, Religious
   Maturity
  -Assoc. Prof., Psychology
   Mankato State Univ.

MILES, Margaret R.
  -13 Shepard St., #5
   Cambridge, MA 02138
  -(617) 495-4565
  -Episcopal
  -Historical Theology, Patristics
  -PhD, Graduate Theo. Union, 1977
  -Augustine on the Body; Ideas of
   Body and Asceticism in Chris-
   tian Theology
  -Asst. Prof., Historical Theology,
   Harvard Divinity School

MOREY-GAINES, Ann-Janine
-Religious Studies Dept.
Southern Illinois Univ.
Carbondale, IL 62901
-(618) 453-3067
-American Religion, American
Literature and Religion, esp.
19th-20th Century
-PhD, Univ. of Southern
California, 1979
-Thesis: Apples and Ashes (Cul-
ture, Metaphor and Morality in
the American Dream)
-Rhetoric of Religion and Sexu-
ality in 19th Century American
Fiction
-Asst. Prof., Southern Illinois
Univ./Carbondale

MUXWORTHY, Diana
-Harvard Divinity School
Cambridge, MA 02138
-Unification Church
-Religion and Culture
-M.Div., Harvard Divinity School,
1981
-Liberation Theology, Dynamics
of Psychology, Psychology and
Religion
-"Offering," in Way of the
World

NORBECK, Elizabeth C.
-Lancaster Theo. Sem.
Lancaster, PA 17603
-(717) 393-0654
-History of American Religions,
New England Puritanism
-PhD, Harvard Univ., 1978
-Pre-Revolutionary Puritanism in
Northern New England, Women's
Studies, 19th Century Congrega-
tionalism
-Asst. Prof., Church History;
Dean of Students,
Lancaster Theo. Sem.

NYITRAY, Vivian-Lee
-Dept. of Religious Studies
Stanford Univ.
Stanford, CA 94305
-(415) 497-3322
-Chinese Religions
-PhD, Stanford Univ., expected
1982
-Thesis: Mirrors of Virtue: Reli-
gious Biography in Early China
-International Programs in the
Republic of China
-Instr., Philosophy,
California State Univ.

O'CONNOR, June E.
-Program in Religious Studies
Univ. of California
Riverside, CA 92521
-(714) 787-3741
-Contemporary Religious Thought,
Religious Ethics
-PhD, Temple Univ., 1973
-The Quest for Political and
Spiritual Liberation: A Study
in the Thought of Sri Aurobindo
Ghose; Ethics and Autobiography,
Liberation Theology, Spiritu-
ality and Sensuality
-Assoc. Prof., Univ. of
California/Riverside

OLIVER, Mary Anne McPherson
-1632 Grant St.
Berkeley, CA 94703
-(415) 843-6618
-Episcopal
-Religion and Culture, Spiritual
Theology, Comparative Literature
-PhD, Graduate Theo. Union/
Berkeley, 1972
-Mystical Experience and Literary
Technique, Taize and Contempla-
tion, Conjugal Spirituality

ORSEN, (Rev.) Sandra D.
-13342 Hart
 Huntington Woods, MI 48070
-(313) 546-7336
-American Lutheran Church
-Preaching, Communications
-D. Min., Andover Newton Theo.
 School, 1980
-Co-pastor, St. Olaf
 Lutheran church, Detroit, MI

PAGE, Patricia N.
-The Church Divinity School
 of the Pacific
 2451 Ridge Rd.
 Berkeley, CA 94709
-(415) 848-3282
-Episcopal
-Religious Education
-PhD, New York Univ., pending
-Thesis: Effect of Several
 Methods of Adult Bible Study on
 Coping Processes
-Assoc. Prof., Education;
 Director of Continuing Education,
 The Church Divinity School of
 the Pacific

PATRICK, Anne E.
-Carleton College
 Northfield, MN 55057
-Roman Catholic
-Religion and Culture, Religion
 and Literature: Theology, Ethics,
 Fiction
-PhD, Univ. of Chicago Divinity
 School, 1980
-Thesis: H. Richard Niebuhr's
 Ethics of Responsibility: A Re-
 source for Literary Criticism
-Conscience--The Use of this Term
 in Theological, Ethical and
 Popular Moral Discourse
-Instr./Asst. Prof., Religion
 Carleton College

PATRICK, Mary W.
-202 S. Garth
 Columbia, MO 65201
-(314) 449-1891
-Disciples of Christ
-New Testament
-PhD, Univ. of Chicago, pending

PEACOCK, Virginia A.
-35 Charles St. W, #203
 Toronto, Ont. M4Y 1R6 CANADA
-Episcopal
-Ethics, Systematics, Biblical
 Studies, Women's Studies
-PhD, Univ. of St. Michael's
 College, pending
-Thesis: Dispositional versus
 Decisional Ethics in the Thought
 of Jonathan Edwards

PENET, (Sr.) Mary Emil, IHM
-Weston School of Theology
 3 Phillips Place
 Cambridge, MA 02138
-(617) 492-1960
-Roman Catholic
-Social Ethics, Property Theory,
 Marxism, Metaethics
-PhD, St. Louis Univ., 1950
-Thesis: Property and Right in
 Representative 13th to 17th
 Century Moralists
-Assoc. Prof., Moral Theology
 and Social Ethics
 Weston School of Theology

PLASKOW, Judith
-64-53 Bell Blvd.
 Bayside, NY 11364
-(212) 423-8739
-Jewish
-Contemporary Religious Thought,
 Women and Religion
-PhD, Yale Univ., 1975
-Womanspirit Rising; Woman and
 Body in Western Religious Thought
-Asst. Prof., Religious Studies,
 Manhattan College

PRAEDER, Susan Marie
-Boston College
Dept. of Theology
Chestnut Hill, MA 02167
-(617) 969-0100
-Roman Catholic
-New Testament, Synoptics, Acts
-PhD, Graduate Theo. Union, 1980
-Thesis: The Narrative Voyage:
An Analysis and Interpretation
of Acts 27-28
-New Testament Narratives,
Christology
-Asst. Prof., Theology,
Boston College

PRELINGER, Catherine M.
-Franklin Papers
1603A Yale Station
New Haven, CT 06520
-(203) 436-8646
-Religion and Culture, German
19th Century Women and Religion
-PhD, Yale Univ., 1954
-Thesis: A Decade of Dissent in
Germany: The Society of Pro-
testant Friends and the German
Catholic Church, 1840-1850
-Religious Radicalism and the
Rise of Feminism in Germany
-Asst. Ed., The Papers of
Benjamin Franklin;
Research Assoc., History,
Yale Univ.

PROCTER-SMITH, Marjorie
-1702 Hildreth
South Bend, IN 46615
-(219) 287-5510
-Episcopal
-Liturgical Studies
-PhD, Univ. of Notre Dame,
expected 1981
-Shaker Worship and Community
Structures, Women and Worship

RABUZZI, Kathryn Allen
-Dept. of English
Syracuse Univ.
Syracuse, NY 13210
-(315) 423-2173
-Religion and Culture
-PhD, Syracuse Univ., 1976
-The Sacred and the Feminine,
forthcoming; Radical Feminist
Theology, Humanities and Medicine
-Research Assoc., Humanities and
Medicine, Upstate Medical Center;
P.T. Instr., English,
Syracuse Univ.

RAGLE, Sandra
-2917 Princeton, #17
Fort Worth, TX 76109
-(817) 924-0206
-Christian Church
(Disciples of Christ)
-Psychology of Religion, The-
ology of Pastoral Care
-M.Div., Brite Divinity School,
pending

RAITT, Jill
-3213 Pickett Rd.
Durham, NC 27705
-(919) 684-3234
-Historical Theology, Women and
Religion, Medieval and Renais-
sance
-PhD, Univ. of Chicago, 1970
-Thesis: The Eucharistic
Thought of Theodore Beza
-Shapers of Traditions in
Germany, Switzerland and
Poland, 1560-1600
-Assoc. Prof., Duke Univ.

RAKOCZY, Susan F.
-5112 Tracy
Kansas City, MO 64110
-(816) 363-5392; 363-3585
-Catholic

RAKOCZY, (cont.)
-Contemporary Religious Thought,
Christian Spirituality
-PhD, Catholic Univ. of America,
1980
-Thesis: The Structures of Dis-
cernment Processes and the
Meaning of Discernment Language
in Published U.S. Catholic Lit-
erature, 1965-1978, An Analysis
-Theology of Discernment, Inte-
gration of Christian Spiritu-
ality and Commitment to
Social Justice
-Staff Member, Center for
Pastoral Ministry, Kansas City

REED, Barbara E.
-School of Religion
Univ. of Iowa
Iowa City, IA 52242
-History of Chinese Religions,
Chinese Buddhism in the Six Dy-
nasties Period
-PhD, Univ. of Iowa, expected
1982
-Thesis: Correspondence Between
Hui-yüan and Kumarajiva
-Teaching-Research Fellow,
Univ. of Iowa

REYNOLDS, Holly Baker
-9 Lovewell Rd.
Wellesley, MA 02181
-(617) 235-1694
-History of Religions, Hinduism --
South Indian
-PhD, Univ. of Wisconsin, 1978
-Women's Religious Life, Women's
Rituals
-Asst. Prof., Wellesley College

RHODES, Lynn N.
-26 Sigourney St.
Jamaica Plain, MA 02130
-(617) 522-2291
-United Methodist
-Church and Ministry, Field Education

RHODES, (cont.)
-ThD, Boston Univ. School of
Theology, expected 1983
-Women in Ministry, Racism,
Urban Ministry
-Asst. Dir., Field Education,
Boston Univ. School of Theology

RICHARDSON, Nancy
-41 Ballard St.
Jamaica Plain, MA 02130
-(617) 524-7142
-United Church of Christ
-Ethics, Religious Education,
Pastoral Practical, Feminist/
Liberation Approaches to Educa-
tion and Change
-PhD, Boston Univ., expected 1984
-Co-author, Your Daughters Shall
Prophesy: Feminist Alternatives
in Theological Education; Rela-
tionship between Languages and
Power
-Dir., Student and Community Life,
Boston Univ. School of Theology

RICHARDSON, Ruth
-Drew Univ.
Madison, NJ 07940
-(201) 966-8093
-19th and 20th Century German
Philosophy and Theology, Con-
temporary European Church His-
tory, Marxism (History and
Theory)
-PhD, Drew Univ., expected 1983
-Thesis: Schleiermacher's
Vertraute Briefe über Lucinde:
Key to the Development of His
Thought
-Community Resources and Crim-
inal Justice, with S. Dobson
and M. Louka; Women in Communion:
A Personal Narrative of Adole-
sence and Old Age (forthcoming)

RINGE, Sharon H.
-Methodist Theo. School in Ohio
Delaware, OH 43015
-(614) 363-1146
-United Church of Christ
-New Testament, Synoptic Gospels
-PhD, Union Theo. Sem., NY, ex-
pected 1981
-Thesis: Jubilee Motifs in the
Ministry and Teaching of Jesus
According to the Synoptic Gospels

ROGERS, Isabel W.
-1205 Palmyra Ave.
Richmond, VA 23227
-(804) 359-5031
-Presbyterian
-Ethics, History of Christian
Thought, Ecology, Women's
Studies
-PhD, Duke Univ., 1961
-In Response to God Sing a New
Song, Our Shared Earth
-Prof., Applied Christianity,
Presbyterian School of Christian
Education

ROSS, Susan A.,
-Dept. of Religious Studies
St. Norbert College
De Pere, WI 54115
-(414) 337-3000
-Contemporary Religious Thought,
Theology, Hermeneutics
-PhD, Univ. of Chicago Divinity
School, pending
-Thesis: Art and Revelation: A
Study of Gadamer, Schillebeeckx,
and von Balthasar
-Art and Religion, Contemporary
Roman Catholic Theology
-Instr., St. Norbert College

RUBIN, Jane
-2732 Derby St.
Berkeley, CA 94705
-(415) 549-1249
-Religious Society of Friends
-Philosophy of Religion, Soci-

RUBIN, (cont.)
ology of Religion, Existen-
tialism, Phenomenology
-D.Phil., Univ. of California,
Berkeley, 1979
-Thesis: Kierkegaard and Heidegger
-Acting Instr., Univ. of
California/Berkeley

RUETHER, Rosemary Radford
-Garrett-Evangelical Theo. Sem.
2121 Sheridan Rd.
Evanston, IL 60201
-(312) 866-3953
-Roman Catholic
-Historical Theology, Patristics,
19th Century, Feminism, Soci-
alism, Liberation Theology,
Jewish-Christian Relations
-PhD, Claremont School of The-
ology, 1965
-Thesis: Gregory of Nazianzus:
Rhetor and Philosopher
-New Woman, New Earth; Religion
and Sexism; Women of Spirit;
Women and Religion: The 19th
Century; Faith and Fratricide;
Liberation Theology; The Radical
Kingdom
-Georgia Harkness Prof. of
Theology, Garrett-Evangelical
Theo. Sem.

RUNNING, Leona Glidden
-89 Fourth St.
Berrien Springs, MI 49103
-(616) 471-1582
-Old Testament, Semitic
Languages
-PhD, Johns Hopkins Univ., 1964
-Thesis: An Investigation of
the Syriac Version of Isaiah
-Prof., Biblical Languages,
Andrews Univ.

RUSSELL, (Sr.) Jane Elyse, OSF
-129 Ash, Apt. 5
Ames, IA 50010
-(515) 292-5442
-Roman Catholic

RUSSELL, Jane (cont.)
-Contemporary Religious Thought,
New Testament, Pastoral The-
ology, Roman Catholic Studies
-PhD, Univ. of Notre Dame, 1980
-Thesis: Renewing the Gospel Com-
munity: Four Catholic Movements
and an Anabaptist Parallel
-Renewal in the Church, Women
and Religion
-Res. Theologian, St. Thomas
Aquinas Church and Catholic
Student Center, Iowa State Univ.

RUSSELL, Letty M.
-409 Prospect St.
New Haven, CT 06510
-(203) 453-6640
-United Presbyterian, U.S.A.
-Theology, Anthropology
-ThD, Union Theo. Sem., NY, 1969
-The Future of Partnership;
Liberation Theologies
-Assoc. Prof., Yale Div. School

SAWICKI, Marianne
-312 S. Carolina Ave., SE
Washington, D.C. 20003
-(202) 546-8967
-Contemporary Religious Thought,
Communications, Language
-PhD, Catholic Univ. of America,
expected 1981
-Faith and Sexism; Liturgy, Sac-
ramental Theology, Heidegger
-Man. Ed., Our Gifts, Catholic
Univ.

SAWIN, Margaret M.
-P.O. Box 8452
Rochester, NY 14618
-(716) 225-9530; 232-3530
-American Baptist
-Family and Religious Education
-EdD, Univ. of Maryland, 1969

SAWIN, (cont.)
-"Family Enrichment with Family
Clusters"; Influence of Family
System on Religious Development
-Free-lance Consultant

SCHATKIN, Margaret A.
-215-05 39th Ave.
Bayside, NY 11361
-(212) 224-5659
-Historical Theology, Patristics
-PhD, Fordham Univ., 1967
-Thesis: St. John Chrysostom as
Apologist
-Co-editor, The Heritage of the
Early Church
-Assoc. Prof., Boston College

SCHIERLING, Marla J.
-913 Lynn Haven
Hazelwood, MO 63042
-(314) 895-1702
-Biblical Languages and Litera-
ture, Women's Studies
-PhD, St. Louis Univ., 1980
-Thesis: Women, Cult, and
Miracle Recital in Mark
-"The Influence of the Ancient
Romances on the Book of Acts"
-Teaching Asst., St. Louis Univ.

SCHMIDT, Jean Miller
-The Iliff School of Theology
2201 S. Univ. Blvd.
Denver, CO 80210
-(303) 744-1287
-Religion and Culture, History
of Christianity
-PhD, Univ. of Chicago, 1969
-Thesis: Evangelical vs. Social
Christianity in American Pro-
testantism
-Assoc. Prof.,
Iliff School of Theology

SCHNEIDER, Mary L.
-4333 W. Willow
Lansing, MI 48917
-(517) 321-4461
-Contemporary Theology,
Religion in American Culture

SCHNEIDER, (cont.)
-PhD, Marquette Univ., 1971
-"American Civil Religion and
the National Catholic Rural Life
Conference," An American Church,
ed. D. Alvarez; Thomas Merton,
Contemporary Ecclesiology
-Assoc. Prof., Michigan State Univ.

SETTA, Susan M.
-485 Washington St.
Brookline, MA 02146
-(617) 731-9458
-American Religion and Culture,
Women in American Religion
-PhD, Penn State Univ., 1979
-Thesis: Woman of the Apocalypse:
The Reincorporation of the Fem-
inine through the Second Coming
of Christ in Ann Lee
-"Denial of the Female, Affirma-
tion of the Feminine: The Mother-
Father God of Mary Baker Eddy"
in Beyond Androcentrism, ed.,
R. Gross; Women and Healing,
Medical Ethics
-Asst. Prof., Northeastern Univ.

SHANKER-RODRIGUEZ, Raj Kumari
-52 Riverbrook
Nepean, Ottawa, Ont., CANADA
-(613) 820-4245
-History of Religions, Hinduism,
Buddhism
-PhD, Sorbonne, Paris, 1972
-Karma-Yoga in the Bhagavadgita,
Aspects and Implications of
Hindu Feminine Theology
-P.T. Prof., Religious Studies ,
Univ. of Ottawa

SHEATS, Mary Boney
-Agnes Scott College
Decatur, GA 30030
-(404) 377-7145
-Presbyterian Church, U.S.
-Old and New Testament, Litera-
ture of Religion
-PhD, Columbia Univ., 1956
-Relation between Testaments,
Place of Women in Biblical

SHEATS, (cont.)
Tradition, Wisdom Literature
-Callaway Prof.,
Agnes Cott College

SHEEHAN, (Sr.) Mary Ellen
-44011 Five Mile
Plymouth, MI 48170
-STD, Louvain, Belgium
-Systematics
-Assoc. Prof.,
St. John's Provincial Sem.

SMITH, Jane Idleman
-45 Francis Ave.
Cambridge, MA 02138
-(617) 495-4514
-United Church of Christ
-History of Religions, Islamics
-PhD, Harvard Univ., 1970
-Thesis: The Concept "Islam" in
History of Qur'anic Exegesis
-Books, reviews, articles, gen-
eral info. to Islam, Women in
Islam
-Assoc. Dean, Academic Affairs;
Lec., History of Religions,
Harvard Divinity School

SMITH, Mary Carroll
-Religion Dept.
Vassar College
Poughkeepsie, NY 12601
-(914) 452-7000 x2214
-Sanskrit, Indian Studies
-PhD, Harvard Univ., 1972
-Articles on Indian Epic; Virgin
Mary and Ancient Goddess;
Reviews
-Asst. Prof., Vassar College

SMITH, Ruth Lynette
-86 Toxteth St.
Brookline, MA 02146
-(617) 738-9416
-Methodist
-Social Ethics, Sociology of
Religion
-PhD, Boston Univ., expected 1981
-Thesis: The Individual and
Society in Reinhold Niebuhr and

SMITH, Ruth (cont.)
  Karl Marx
  -Dept. of Religion and Society,
  Andover Newton Theo. School

SPENCER, Aida Besançon
  -V-1 Seminary Village
  Louisville, KY 40207
  -(502) 897-7018
  -United Presbyterian, U.S.A.
  -New Testament, Exegesis
  -PhD, Southern Baptist Theo.
  Sem., expected 1982

SPIELMAN, Bethany
  -801 10th Ave.
  Coralville, IA
  -(319) 351-2477
  -Lutheran
  -Ethics, Bioethics
  -PhD, Univ. of Iowa, expected
  1982
  -Teaching Asst., Univ. of Iowa

SQUIRE, Anne M.
  -731 Weston Dr.
  Ottawa, Ont., CANADA
  -(613) 231-3863
  -United Church of Canada
  -Women in Religion
  -DD, United Theo. College, 1980
  -Women in the Church
  -Lect., Carleton Univ.

STAPLETON, Carolyn L.
  -Box 452
  Southern Methodist Univ.
  Dallas, TX 75275
  -(214) 363-9107
  -United Methodist
  -History of Religions, American
  Church History
  -D.Min., Southern Methodist
  Univ., expected 1981
  -Articles on Women and Religion,
  Protestant Women in 19th and
  20th Century America

STARKEY, Peggy
  -Dept. of Religion
  Meredith College
  Raleigh, NC 27611
  -United Methodist
  -Theology of World Religion,
  Contemporary Religious Thought
  -PhD, Union Theo. Sem., 1978
  -Thesis: Salvation as a Problem
  in Christian Theology of Reli-
  gions
  -Asst. Prof., Meredith College

STEINBERG, Naomi
  -99 Claremont Ave., Apt. 211
  New York, NY 10027
  -(212) 666-4836
  -Old Testament
  -PhD, Columbia Univ., expected
  1981
  -Thesis: Adam and Eve's Daughters
  are Many: Sex Differentiated
  Role Action in Ancient Israelite
  Society

STEWART, Mary Zeiss
  -1005 Illinois St.
  Mt. Pleasant, MI 48858
  -Religion and Culture, Religion
  and Literature
  -PhD, Syracuse Univ., 1980
  -Autobiography, Myth and Psyche,
  Story, Women's Studies, Depth
  Psychology
  -Instr., Religion
  Central Michigan Univ.

STOKES, G. Allison
  -80 Rimmon Rd.
  Woodbridge, CT 06525
  -(203) 397-2268
  -United Church of Christ
  -American Religious History,
  Religion and Psychology
  -PhD, Yale Univ., pending
  -Thesis: The Rise of Religion
  and Health Movement in American
  Protestantism, 1906-1945
  -Biography of H. Flanders Dunbar

SWANER, Ann Feeley
-42 Deerfield Common
Iowa City, IA 52240
-(319) 351-0882
-Ethics, Ethics of Sexuality
and Family Life
-PhD, Univ. of Iowa, expected
1982
-Teaching Asst., Univ. of Iowa

TEKEL, Rose M.
-Simone de Beauvoir Institute
Concordia Univ.
Montreal, Que. H4B 1R6 CANADA
-(514) 879-8521
-Jewish
-Sociology of Religion, Compara-
tive Ethics
-PhD, Concordia Univ., pending
-Thesis: Changing Definitions of
Motherhood in Catholic and
Jewish Periodicals, 1965-1975
-Women in Western Religions,
Religious Development of
Children, Women and Power
-Lect., Concordia Univ.

TETLOW, Elisabeth M.
-2218 Napoleon Ave.
New Orleans, LA 70115
-(504) 891-2641
-Roman Catholic
-New Testament
-STM, Woodstock College, 1974
-Women and Ministry in the New
Testament; NT Theology of Mar-
riage, Spirituality
-Lect., Loyola Univ. of
New Orleans

TIMBIE, Janet
-4608 Merivale Rd.
Chevy Chase, MD 20015
-(301) 657-8326
-History of Christian Thought,
Christianity in Egypt
-PhD, Univ. of Pennsylvania, 1979
-Development of Monasticism in
Upper Egypt, Life and Works of
Shenoute of Atripe
-Mellon Fellow,
Catholic Univ. of America

TOLANDER, (Rev.) Marie
-Still Waters
Henniker, NH 03242
-(603) 428-7159
-United Church of Christ
-Religious Education, The
Pastorate
-M.Div., Andover Newton Theo.
School, 1974
-Laity Training, Christian Edu-
cation
-Founder, Dir., "Still Waters,"
A Christian Resources Center;
Assoc. Pastor,
Brookside Cong. Church

UMANSKY, Ellen M.
-Dept. of Religion
Princeton Univ.
Princeton, NJ 08540
-(609) 452-4481
-Jewish
-Modern Judaism
-PhD, Columbia Univ., 1981
-Thesis: Lily H. Montagu and the
Development of Liberal Judaism
in England
-Women in Judaism
-Lect., Religion, Princeton Univ.

$\mathcal{V}$

VATER, Ann M.
-Dept. of Philosophy and
Religious Studies
Western Illinois Univ.
Macomb, IL 61455
-(309) 298-1057; 837-3407
-Roman Catholic
-Hebrew Scripture/Old Testament,
Form Criticism
-PhD, Yale Univ., 1976
-"The Communication of Messages
and Oracles as a Narration
Medium in the O.T."; Sabbath,
Divine Female Wisdom
-Asst. Prof.,
Western Illinois Univ.

VOISIN, Carol Jean
-Graduate Theo. Union
2465 Le Conte
Berkeley, CA 94709
-(415) 841-9811
-Contemporary Religious Thought,
Systematic Theology
-ThD, Graduate Theo. Union, 1980
-Thesis: Schleiermacher's Treat-
ment of the Trinity: Exploring
the Implications of the Trinity
as the Keystone of Christian
Faith
-Human Sexuality, God Talk, The-
ology of Ecology

$\mathcal{W}$

WAKEMAN, Mary K.
-208½ Leftwich St.
Greensboro, NC 27401
-(919) 275-4857
-History of Religions, Old Testament, Near Eastern, Judaic
Studies

WAKEMAN, (cont.)
-PhD, Brandeis Univ., 1969
-God's Battle with the Monster:
A Study in Biblical Imagery;
From Goddess to God through the
Pantheons of Ancient Cities
-Assoc. Prof., Religious Studies,
Univ. of North Carolina

WALLACE, M. Elizabeth
-178 E. Green St.
Westminster, MD 21157
-(301) 848-2703
-Religion and Culture, Religion
and Literature/Writing
-PhD, Univ. of Kent at Canterbury,
1975
-Thesis: Epistemology: Literature
and Religion as Knowledge
-D.H. Lawrence, Michael Polanyi,
20th Century American Women
Writers of the South
-Asst. Prof.,
Gettysburg College, PA

WALTON, Janet R., SNJM
-527 Riverside Dr.
New York, NY 10027
-(212) 622-3342
-Roman Catholic
-Religion and Culture; Worship,
Music and the Arts
-EdD, Columbia Univ., 1979
-Thesis: Aesthetic Contributions
to Liturgical Renewal
-The Interrelationship of the
Arts, Aesthetics and the Ex-
perience of Worship
-Asst. Prof., Worship,
Union Theo. Sem., NY

WEDDINGTON, Diane
-2451 Ridge Rd.
Berkeley, CA 94709
-(415) 548-7825
-Episcopal

WEDDINGTON, (cont.)
-Labor Law, Bioethics, Professional Ethics
-PhD, Graduate Theo. Union, expected 1982
-Journalism, Theory of Film
-Staff, National Catholic Reporter

WEISMAN, Celia Behrman
-304 E. 90th St., #5C
New York, NY 10028
-(212) 534-2266
-Religion and the Arts
-PhD, Columbia Univ., pending
-Feminist Studies in Religion and Arts, Women's Rituals
-Teaching Asst., Columbia Univ.

WEHR, Demaris
-502 Walnut Lane
Swarthmore, PA 19081
-(215) 328-4680
-Psychology and Religion
-Phd, Temple Univ., 1981
-Thesis: Jungian Psychology and Feminist Theology: Compatible or Incompatible Models of Self-Actualization

WISKOCHIL, Marilyn Salmon
-455 Craig Rd.
Cincinnati, OH 45220
-(513) 528-2841
-American Lutheran Church
-Old Testament
-PhD, Hebrew Union College, OH, pending
-History of Interpretation

YOSHIOKA, Barbara S.
-P.O. Box 220
Smith River, CA 95567
-(707) 487-7301
-Religion and Culture
-PhD, Syracuse Univ., 1977
-Pres., United Lily Growers, Inc.

YOUNG, Pamela Dickey
-204 Moore Hall
Southern Methodist Univ.
Dallas, TX 75275
-(214) 361-8874
-United Church of Canada
-Contemporary Religious Thought, Systematic Theology
-PhD, Southern Methodist Univ., pending
-Thesis: A Priori Christianity: A Study Based on the Theology of Karl Rahner

ZIKMUND, Barbara Brown
-Pacific School of Religion
1798 Scenic Ave.
Berkeley, CA 94709
-United Church of Christ
-History of Christian Thought
-PhD, Duke Univ., 1969
-American Religious Experiment, ed. with Clyde Manochrick; Women in the United Church of Christ
-Academic Dean, Pacific School of Religion

ZOSSO, Terisse SSpS
-Divine Word College
 Epworth, IA 52045
-(319) 876-3362
-Roman Catholic
-Psychology of Religion
-PhD, Marquette Univ., 1976
-Thesis: Ethics of the Spirit:
 Haering and Loevinger
-Spiritual Growth and Development
-Instr., Divine Word College

ZULKOWSKY, Patricia A.
-School of Theology
 Box 334
 Claremont, CA 91711
-(714) 624-6952
-Unification Church
-Psychology and Religion, Reli-
 gious Education
-MA and PhD, Pastoral Counseling,
 School of Theology at Claremont,
 pending
-Marriage Counseling in the Uni-
 fication Church

INDEX BY FIELD

AMERICAN RELIGIOUS HISTORY AND
  CULTURE

Albanese, Catherine L.
Alpert, Rebecca Trachtenberg
Athans, Marty Christine, BVM
Bass, Dorothy C.
Boyd, Sandra H.
Braude, Ann
Crosthwaite, Jane F.
Dillenberger, Jane
Fishburn, Janet F.
Hostetler, Beulah S.
Keller, Rosemary Skinner
Killen, Patricia O'Connell
Kujawa, Sheryl A.
Lindley, Susan Hill
Morey-Gaines, Ann-Janine
Nordbeck, Elizabeth C.
Schneider, Mary L.
Setta, Susan M.
Stapleton, Carolyn L.
Stokes, G. Allison
Zikmund, Barbara Brown

ANTHROPOLOGY AND SOCIOLOGY OF
  RELIGION

Bancroft, Nancy
Brenneman, Mary G.
Brown, Karen McCarthy
Furman, Frida Kerner
Haywood, Carol Lois
Hiatt, (Rev.) Suzanne R.
Jay, Nancy B.
Jonte, Diane E.
Lummis, Adair T.
Rubin, Jane
Russell, Letty M.
Smith, Ruth Lynette
Tekel, Rose M.

BIBLICAL AND NEAR EASTERN STUDIES

Edwards, (Rev.) Sarah A.
Foley, M. Nadine, OP
Harris, Rivkah
Howe, E. Margaret
Koehler, Joan, SSSF
Maurer, M. Sylvia, CSC
Peacock, Virginia A.
Wakeman, Mary K.

CONTEMPORARY RELIGIOUS THOUGHT

Bloomquist, Karen L.
Carr, Anne
Christ, Carol P.
Cooey-Nichols, Paula Martin
Cossette, Ann d.
Croke, Prudence Mary, OSM
Dooley, Anne Mary, SSJ
Earley, Margaret
Foley, M. Nadine, OP
Getz, Lorine M.
Going, Cathleen M.
Goosen, Marilyn M.
Hammett, Jenny Y.
Harrington, Patricia A.
Haydock, Ann S.
Kinschner, Julia
Mallory, Mary Peter, CSJ
O'Connor, June E.
Plaskow, Judith
Rakoczy, Susan F.
Richardson, Ruth
Ross, Susan A.
Ruether, Rosemary Radford
Russell (Sr.) Jane Elyse, OSF
Swicki, Marianne
Starkey, Peggy
Young, Pamela Dickey

CHURCH AND MINISTRY

Bozeman, (Rev.) Jean
Falls, Helen E.
Hiatt, (Rev.) Suzanne R.
Leaming, (Rev.) Marjorie Newlin
Lummis, Adair T.
Orsen (Rev.) Sandra D.
Procter-Smith, Marjorie
Rhodes, Lynn N.
Walton, Janet R. SNJM

CHURCH HISTORY, HISTORY OF CHRISTIANITY, AND HISTORY OF CHRISTIAN ORIGINS

Anda, Eva
Athans, Mary Christine, BVM
Atkinson, Clarissa Webster
Barstow, Anne
Bozak, Lillian C.
Burgess, Faith E.
Clark, Elizabeth A.
Darling, Robin
Deleeuw, Patricia E.
Douglass, Jane Dempsey
Idziak, Janine Marie
Karwedsky, Linda Schleicher
Kujawa, Sheryl A.
Landes, Paula Frederiksen
Lewis, Eleanor V.
Lindley, Susan Hill
Matter, E. Ann
McGinty, Mary Peter, CSJ
McWilliam-Dewart, Joanne
Miles, Margaret R.
Raitt, Jill
Rogers, Isabel W.
Stapleton, Carolyn L.
Timbie, Janet
Zikmund, Barbara Brown

EAST ASIAN

Basu, Patricia Lyons
Breuinin, Arlene Mazak
Feldhaus, Anne
Finaly, Ellison Banks
Gross, Rita M.
Nyitray, Vivian-Lee
Reed, Barbara E.

ETHICS

Andolsen, Barbara Hilkert
Bancroft, Nancy
Cahill, Lisa Sowle
Davis, Dena S.
Dumais, Monique
Furman, Frida Kerner
Gorman, Margaret
Gudorf, Christine E.
Holler, Linda
Idziak, Janine Marie
Jung, Patricia B.
Keller, Rosemary Skinner
Lebacqz, Karen
O'Connor, June E.
Peacock, Virginia A.
Penet, (Sr.) Mary Emil, IHM
Richardson, Nancy
Rogers, Isabel W.
Smith, Ruth Lynette
Spielman, Bethany
Swaner, Ann Feeley
Tekel, Rose M.
Weddington, Diane

HISTORY OF RELIGIONS, WORLD RELIGIONS, COMPARATIVE RELIGIONS

Albanese, Catherine L.
Barstow, Anne
Bass, Dorothy C.
Boyd, Sandra H.
Braude, Ann
Breuinin, Arlene Mazak
Buckley, Jorunn Jacobsen
Cox, Patricia L.
Darling, Robin
Dimmitt, Cornelia
Falk, Nancy Ellen Auer
Feldhaus, Anne
Finaly, Ellison Banks
Fontaine, Carole R.
Haddad, Yvonne Yazbeck
Killen, Patricia O'Connell
King, Sallie B.
Kraemer, Ross S.
Landes, Paula Frederiksen
McDonough, Marie Mahnken
McDonough, Sheila
Reynolds, Holly Baker
Shanker-Rodriquez, Raj Kumari

HISTORY OF RELIGIONS, WORLD
RELIGIONS, COMPARATIVE RELIGIONS
(cont.)

Smith, Jane Idleman
Stapleton, Carolyn L.
Starkey, Peggy
Wakeman, Mary K.

INDIAN/ISLAM

Breuinin, Arlene Mazak
Fontaine, Carole R.
Haddad, Yvonne Yazbeck
McDonough, Sheila
Smith, Jane Idleman
Smith, Mary Carroll

JUDAICA

Alpert, Rebecca Trachtenberg
Birnbaum, Ruth
Edelman, Alice Chasan
Elwell, Ellen Sue Levi
Umansky, Ellen M.

NEW TESTAMENT

Barta, Karen A.
Boucher, Madeleine
Brooten, Bernadetta Joan
Edwards, (Rev.) Sarah A.
Fiorenza, Elizabeth Schüssler
Gaventa, Beverly Roberts
Harris, E. Lynn
Howe, E. Margaret
Kearney, Suzanne M., CSJ
Kroeger, Catherine Clark
Lund, Shirley
Malbon, Elizabeth Struthers
Patrick, Mary W.
Praeder, Susan Marie
Ringe, Sharon H.
Russell, (Sr.) Jane Elyse, OSF
Schierling, Marla J.
Spencer, Aida Besarçon
Tetlow, Elisabeth M.

OLD TESTAMENT AND HEBREW SCRIPTURES

Ahl, Sally W.
Bailey-Adams, Marcy
Buchwald, Lynne S.
Exum, J. Cheryl
Follis, Elaine R.
Fontaine, Carole R.
Harris, E. Lynn
Howell, Maribeth
Laffey, Alice L.
McHatten, Mary Timothy, OP
Running, Leona Glidden
Sheats, Mary Boney
Steinberg, Naomi
Vater, Ann M.
Wiskochil, Marilyn Salmon

PHILOSOPHY OF RELIGION

Alpern, Barbara D.
Cooey-Nichols, Paula Martin
Crunkleton, Martha
Davaney, Sheila Greeve
Douglass, Jane Dempsey
Dumais, Monique
Dunn, Rose Ellen
Foley, M. Nadine, OP
Hammett, Jenny Y.
Idziak, Janine Marie
King, Sallie B.
Richardson, Ruth
Rubin, Jane

RELIGION AND THE ARTS

Clark, Linda J.
Dillenberger, Jane
Getz, Lorine M.
Weisman, Celia Behrman

RELIGION AND CULTURE/SOCIETY

Agnew, Mary Barbara
Bailey-Adams, Marcy
Christ, Carol P.
Crosthwaite, Jane F.

RELIGION AND CULTURE/SOCIETY (cont.)

Culp, Mildred L.
Deconcini, Barbara
Downing, Chris
Fischer, Clare B.
Getz, Lorine M.
Hostetler, Beulah S.
Keller, Rosemary Skinner
Lunz, Elisabeth
McCollum, Adele Brannon
Muxworthy, Diana
Oliver, Mary Anne McPherson
Patrick, Anne E.
Prelinger, Catherine M.
Rabuzzi, Kathryn Allen
Schmidt, Jean Miller
Stewqrt, Mary Zeiss
Wallace, M. Elizabeth
Walton, Janet R., SNJM
Yoshioka, Barbara S.

RELIGION AND LITERATURE

Alpern, Barbara d.
Christ, Carol P.
Culp, Mildred L.
Deconcini, Barbara
Getz, Lorine M.
Morley-Gaines, Ann-Janine
Patrick, Anne E.
Stewart, Mary Zeiss
Wallace, M. Elizabeth

RELIGION AND PSYCHOLOGY/COUNSELING

Babinski, Jeri Drum
Bohn, Carole R.
Chambers, Bessie
Doherty, Anne Mary, SSJ
Foster, Leila M.
Goldenberg, Naomi R.
Gorman, Margaret
Hammett, Jenny Y.
Haydock, Ann S.
Jancoski, Loretta
Jonte, Diane E.
Kehoe, Nancy Clare, RSCJ
Kinschner, Julia
Marks, Patricia Lynne

RELIGION AND PSYCHOLOGY/COUNSELING (cont.)

McCandless, Bardarah
McCollum, Adele Brannon
Meadow, Mary Jo
Ragle, Sandra
Stokes, G. Allison
Wehr, Demaris
Zosso, Terisse, SspS
Zukowsky, Patricia

RELIGIOUS EDUCATION/RELIGION AND EDUCATION

Borchert, Doris Ann
Bozeman, (Rev.) Jean
Butler, (Sr.) Sara
Congdon-Martin, (Rev.) Elizabeth W.
Croke, Prudence Mary, OSM
Croteau-Chonka, Clarisse D.
Crouch, Jacqueline, SM
Elwell, Ellen Sue Levi
Gorman, Margaret
Harris, E. Lynn
Harris, Eleanor
Harris, Maria
Kluepfel, Marie Patricia McIntyre
Koller-Fox, Cherie
Leaming, (Rev.) Marjorie Newlin
Marks, Patricia Lynne
McCandless, Bardarah
Page, Patricia N.
Richardson, Nancy M.
Tolander, (Rev.) Marie
Zulkowsky, Patricia A.

THEOLOGY: CONTEMPORARY

Bloomquist, Karen L.
Daveney, Sheila Greeve
heyward, I. Carter
Schneider, Mary L.
Voisin, Carol Jean

THEOLOGY: GENERAL

Belmonte, Frances
Buckley, Mary I.

THEOLOGY: GENERAL (cont.)

Dreyer, Elizabeth
Dumais, Monique
Gleason, M. Elizabeth, CSJ
Griffin, (Sr.) Isabel Mary
Kluepfel, Marie Patricia McIntyre
Livezey, Lois Gehr
Russell, Letty M.
Starkey, Peggy

THEOLOGY: HISTORICAL

Atkinson, Clarissa Webster
Belmonte, Frances
Cardman, Francine Jo
Cunningham, (Sr.) Agnes, SSCM
Earley, Margaret
Greeley, Dolores, RSM
Miles, Margaret R.
Raitt, Jill
Richardson, Ruth
Ruether, Rosemary Radford
Schatkin, Margaret A.

THEOLOGY: PASTORAL/PRACTICAL

Bohn, Carole R.
Campbell, Laetitia A., OP
Chambers, Bessie
Clark, Linda J.
Congdon, Martin, (Rev.) Elizabeth W.
Croteau-Chronka, Clarisse D.
Crouch, Jacqueline, SM
Curtis, (Rev.) Jean G.
Doherty, Anne
Falls, Helen E.
Fiorenza, Elizabeth Schüssler
Harris, Maria
Hiatt, (Rev.) Suzanne R.
Jancoski, Loretta
Kehoe, Nancy Clare, RSCJ
Ragle, Sandra
Zulkowsky, Patricia A.

THEOLOGY: SYSTEMATIC

Belmonte, Frances
Bloomquist, Karen L.

THEOLOGY: SYSTEMATIC (cont.)

Buckley, Mary I.
Butler, (Sr.) Sara
Cossette, Ann D.
Croke, Prudence Mary, OSM
Earley, Margaret
Getz, Lorine M.
Greeley, Dolores, RSM
Heyward, I. Carter
Hunter, Mary E.
Kinschner, Julia
Peacock, Virginia A.
Sheehan, (Sr.) Mary Ellen
Stapleton, Carolyn L.
Voisin, Carol Jean
Young, Pamela Dickey

WOMEN"S STUDIES

Anda, Eva
Andolsen, Barbara Hilkert
Barstow, Anne
Brooten, Bernadetta Joan
Christ, Carol P.
Clark, Elizabeth A.
Davaney, Sheila Greeve
Downing, Chris
Falk, Nancy Ellen Auer
Getz, Lorine M.
Goldenberg, Naomi R.
Gross, Rita M.
Haydock, Ann S.
Haywood, Carol Lois
Heyward, I. Carter
Hiatt, (Rev.) Suzanne R..
Hunt, Mary E.
Jonte, Diane E.
Karwedsky, Linda Schleicher
Kujawa, Sheryl A.
Leaming, (Rev.) Marjorie Newlin
Lunz, Elisabeth
Mccollum, Adele Brannon
McDonough, Marie Mahnken
McDonough, Sheila
Peacock, Virginia
Plaskow, Judith
Prelinger, Catherine M.
Raitt, Jill
Reynolds, Holly Baker
Rhodes, Lynn N.

WOMEN'S STUDIES (cont.)

Richardson, Nancy
Ruether, Rosemary Radford
Russell, Letty M.
Sawicki, Marianne
Schmidt, Jean Miller
Setta, Susan M.
Squire, Anne M.
Stewart, Mary Zeiss
Tekel, Rose M.
Wehr, Demaris
Weisman, Celia Behrman
Young, Pamela Dickey

WOMEN'S CAUCUS: RELIGIOUS STUDIES

REGISTRY INFORMATION

NAME: _____ PHONE: _____

ADDRESS: _____

_____

REL. AFFILIATION/ORDINATION STATUS (opt.): _____

FIELD (number in order of importance up to 4 of the following
    areas beginning with 1 . . .)

_____	Amer. Religion	Anthro. of Rel. _____
_____	Arts, Literature & Religion	Cont. Rel. Thought _____
_____	Eastern Religions	Ethics
_____	Hebrew Scriptures	Historical Theo. _____
_____	History of Religions	Islam
_____	Judaica	Liberation Theo. _____
_____	New Testament	Pastoral Theo.
_____	Phil. of Rel.	Psychology of Rel. _____
_____	Rel. & Cult./Soc.	Religious Ed.
_____	Sociology of Rel.	Systematic Theo. _____
_____	Women/Feminist Studies	Other _____

LAST DEGREE, DATE AND _____
        INSTITUTION: _____

THESIS: _____
        _____

PUBLISHED WORKS: _____

_____

_____

PRESENT APPT./INSTITUTION: _____

CURRENT RESEARCH PROJECT: _____

* * *

MAIL COMPLETED FORMS TO:

Registry of Women in Religious Studies
c/o The Edwin Mellen Press
P.O. Box 450
Lewiston, New York 14092

WOMEN'S CAUCUS: RELIGIOUS STUDIES

REGISTRY INFORMATION

NAME: _____ PHONE: _____

ADDRESS: _____

_____

REL. AFFILIATION/ORDINATION STATUS (opt.): _____

FIELD (number in order of importance up to 4 of the following
       areas beginning with 1 . . .)

_____	Amer. Religion	Anthro. of Rel.	_____
_____	Arts, Literature & Religion	Cont. Rel. Thought	_____
_____	Eastern Religions	Ethics	
_____	Hebrew Scriptures	Historical Theo.	_____
_____	History of Religions	Islam	
_____	Judaica	Liberation Theo.	_____
_____	New Testament	Pastoral Theo.	
_____	Phil. of Rel.	Psychology of Rel.	_____
_____	Rel. & Cult./Soc.	Religious Ed.	
_____	Sociology of Rel.	Systematic Theo.	_____
_____	Women/Feminist Studies	Other _____	_____

LAST DEGREE, DATE AND _____
          INSTITUTION: _____

THESIS: _____

_____

PUBLISHED WORKS: _____

_____

_____

PRESENT APPT./INSTITUTION: _____

CURRENT RESEARCH PROJECT: _____

* * *

MAIL COMPLETED FORMS TO:

Registry of Women in Religious Studies
c/o The Edwin Mellen Press
P.O. Box 450
Lewiston, New York 14092